D1714153

DISABLED WITCHCRAFT

90 RITUALS FOR
LIMITED-SPOON
PRACTITIONERS

KANDI ZELLER

Microcosm Publishing
Portland, Ore | Cleveland, Ohio

DISABLED WITCHCRAFT: 90 RITUALS FOR LIMITED-SPOON PRACTITIONERS

© Kandi Zeller, 2024
© This edition Microcosm Publishing 2024
First edition - 3,000 copies - September 17, 2024
ISBN 9781648414305
This is Microcosm # 929
Cover by Lindsey Cleworth
Edited by Olivia Rollins

Design by Joe Biel

To join the ranks of high-class stores that feature
Microcosm titles, talk to your rep: In the U.S. COMO (Atlantic), ABRAHAM
(Midwest), BOB BARNETT (Texas, Oklahoma, Arkansas, Louisiana), IMPRINT
(Pacific), TURNAROUND (UK), UTP/MANDA (Canada), NEWSOUTH (Australia/
New Zealand), Observatoire (Africa, Europe), IPR (Middle East), Yvonne Chau
(Southeast Asia), HarperCollins (India), Everest/B.K. Agency (China), Tim Burland
(Japan/Korea), and FAIRE and EMERALD in the gift trade.

For a catalog, write or visit:
Microcosm Publishing
2752 N Williams Ave.
Portland, OR 97227

All the news that's fit to print at www.Microcosm.Pub/Newsletter.

Get more copies of this book at www.Microcosm.Pub/DisabledWitch.

For more witchy books, visit www.Microcosm.Pub/Witchy.

Did you know that you can buy our books directly from us at sliding scale rates?
Support a small, independent publisher and pay less than Amazon's price at **www.
Microcosm.Pub.**

Global labor conditions are bad, and our roots in industrial Cleveland in the '70s and
'80s made us appreciate the need to treat workers right. Therefore, our books are
MADE IN THE USA.

Library of Congress Cataloging-in-Publication Data

Names: Zeller, Kandi, 1995- author.

Title: Disabled witchcraft : 90 rituals for limited-spoon practitioners /
by Kandi Zeller.

Description: Portland : Microcosm Publishing, [2024] | Summary: "Magick is
all around us and should be for everyone, but the practices in many
witchcraft books can be difficult for many of us to perform due to
chronic illnesses, sensory issues, allergies, or other disabilities-and
the financial limitations that often go hand in hand with them. In this
guide, disabled witch Kandi Zeller sets out to change that"-- Provided
by publisher.

Identifiers: LCCN 2024023019 | ISBN 9781648414305

Subjects: LCSH: Witchcraft. | People with disabilities.

Classification: LCC BF1571 .Z45 2024 | DDC 133.4/3--dc23/eng/20240624

LC record available at https://lccn.loc.gov/2024023019

MICROCOSM · PUBLISHING

MICROCOSM PUBLISHING is Portland's most diversified publishing house and distributor, with a focus on the colorful, authentic, and empowering. Our books and zines have put your power in your hands since 1996, equipping readers to make positive changes in their lives and in the world around them. Microcosm emphasizes skill-building, showing hidden histories, and fostering creativity through challenging conventional publishing wisdom with books and bookettes about DIY skills, food, bicycling, gender, self-care, and social justice. What was once a distro and record label started by Joe Biel in a drafty bedroom was determined to be *Publishers Weekly*'s fastest-growing publisher of 2022 and #3 in 2023 and 2024, and is now among the oldest independent publishing houses in Portland, OR, and Cleveland, OH. We are a politically moderate, centrist publisher in a world that has inched to the right for the past 80 years.

Contents

Chapter Three: Nature Rituals • 43

Chapter Four: A Disabled Wheel of the Year • 59

Chapter Five: Thrifty, Scrappy Rituals • 79

Chapter Six: Artistic Rituals • 93

Introduction

Witchcraft Is for Everyone: A Flexible Spiritual Practice for Disabled People

itchcraft is for everyone. That's one of the things I love most about witchcraft as spiritual practice: it is a flexible road, typically walked by the marginalized in resistance to unjust power structures (including religious structures).

As a person who is disabled (at least in part due to religious trauma and abuse), queer, and an eclectic witch, I'm no stranger to that road. I invite my fellow witchy, disabled spoonies[1] on this journey through 90 rituals that are designed to be just as fabulously flexible, irreverent, and sacred as so many witches and other practitioners on the margins who have chosen similar paths of spiritual resistance throughout history. The rituals in this book honor and celebrate disability; they are also financially accessible and adaptable to whatever your circumstances are.

Regardless of sexual orientation, gender identity or expression, religious or spiritual label (or lack thereof), socioeconomic status, race, ability, or any other factor, you are welcome here.

---

1 Those who don't have the same energy and emotional and physical resources as non-disabled people

You are witchy enough.

When you have the spoons, let us walk this path together.

Disability, Witchcraft, and Why I Wrote This Book

To be disabled is to resist by your very existence. My disabled body smashes ableist assumptions in all spiritual spaces. In fact, I believe disability is itself a form of witchcraft.

Why? Because I personally define witchcraft as anything that connects me or others—in a transformative way—to divine love and community, whether I understand that community to be with God/Goddess, saints, those who have gone before, those who will come after, other humans or creatures in the present, the universe, or some combination of the above. And if witchcraft is about transformational connection, my mind goes straight to the way disability interrupts—and offers the opportunity to transform—unjust societal structures by its very presence.

A system like capitalism that demands people all work forty hours per week (or more) at a set location, just to survive and pay their bills? Disability says no.

A society that views healthcare as a luxury for those who can afford it, rather than a human right? Disability says no.

A public place that isn't accessible to people of all abilities and mobilities? Disability says no.

Disability says, "We're here." Disability says, "Everyone will one day be disabled, and many of us are already disabled and can't mask or perform ability at the expense of our bodies any longer."

Witchcraft gives me a why, an undergirding love, a transformative fire of justice to bring to the systems we presently exist in. At its best, witchcraft (and spirituality in general) aligns us with the voices—past, present, and future—on the margins. For me, witchcraft has been a way to transform my experience (and the meaning I make of it) without directly relying on the unjust systems surrounding me. But that doesn't mean, as a disabled person, that I always have access to all parts of the craft.

And when I talk about access, I'm referring in part to financial access. We live in a capitalist society. Even spiritual practices and medical care are monetized and often financially out of reach for many of us, especially those of us who are disabled. And, unfortunately, despite how inclusive witchy spaces can be, witchcraft books don't often address the barriers to access created by capitalism and ableism. A disabled witch is left to ask, What if I have severe allergies and can't do traditional incense? What if my medical bills are so high that I can barely afford any witchy shit?

It's questions like these that have led me to write this book, with a special focus on financial accessibility for disabled witches who find themselves with limited resources amid the swirl of unjust systems that surround us.

As a disabled witch, I've had to cobble together a form of the craft that works for me, in spaces that have often been ableist and financially inaccessible, and I want others to have an easier time on their paths. I live with several disabilities, including but not limited to severe allergies, arthritis, migraines, PTSD, endometriosis, interstitial cystitis, vaginismus/vulvodynia, GERD, dyscalculia, and probable AuDHD (working on a diagnosis for that one at the moment). For these reasons, I'm writing this book for my fellow witchy spoonies who are in search of anti-capitalist, inclusive, and sometimes spicy rituals (with a side of humor and heart).

In hopes that you won't have to be as scrappy but will remain resourceful . . .

In hopes that the craft will become more inclusive and expansive . . .

In hopes that you'll know both snark and reverence are part of the wonder . . .

In hopes that you'll find in the craft another way to resist . . .

In hopes that you'll know the earthy, watery,
windy, fiery power that is magickal you.

That's right. You are fucking magickal.

Some Notes on Language and Inclusivity

There is a conversation within the disability community (and the wider social justice community) regarding whether, as a community, we should use person-first constructions ("person with X disability") or identity-first language ("disabled person") as an expression of disability pride. For myself, I prefer the latter (and will be using that language throughout the book), but I always recommend you ask any individual how they prefer to be referred to. The disabled experience is not monolithic.

Which brings me to another matter of language. I use the word *spoonie* throughout this book. If you're disabled, you're probably no stranger to spoon theory, originally developed by Christine Miserandino to describe her energy levels while living with lupus.[2] Every day, there is an allotment of energy to do tasks; in spoon theory, this energy is represented by spoons lined up on a table. Basically, disabled people have fewer spoons than non-disabled people do.

Disabled people also have another problem: sometimes tasks that cost one spoon for a non-disabled person might cost significantly more spoons for a disabled person.

---

2 You can find Christine Miserandino's original 2003 essay on spoon theory here: butyoudontlooksick.com/articles/written-by-christine/the-spoon-theory/

I live with a number of invisible disabilities, and that is where a lot of spoon discourse lives. However, the term *spoonie* is more inclusive than that. I love how Shruti Chopra of All Things Endometriosis defines this word so inclusively: "A spoonie is a person who is battling an illness, it can be acute, chronic or life-threatening."[3] She writes that the term refers to anyone "with limited amounts of spoons to use each day."

Simply put, whether your disabilities are visible or invisible, I contend that you are included in the word *spoonie*.

I will also note here that I can only speak from my own lived experiences, as most of my disabilities aren't (typically) visible. While I've tried to make each ritual in this book as inclusive as possible, I know I'm going to miss some things about disabilities I haven't experienced, and for that, I am sorry. With this book, I'm hoping to start a conversation, not end it. As you engage with the rituals, please remember that they are all flexible and can be adapted to meet your individual accessibility needs.

Additionally, it should be noted that many of my own disabilities stem from religious trauma. Because that is my experience, religious trauma will come up occasionally; but this book, like witchcraft, is for everyone—including people of all faiths or no faiths or something in between.

Keeping all this in mind, throughout this book, please leave what doesn't serve you. Reclaim and transform what

3 allthingsendometriosis.com/what-is-spoonie-spoon-theory/#google_vignette

you find here. This book of rituals is a conversation, not a rulebook. You are welcome here.

Who Is This Book For?

Witches of all levels are welcome, and of course, this book is for all disabled witches. I've done my best to include information throughout the book that will empower you to learn more and expand your craft in accessible ways.

If you're new to the craft, be aware that I will be using some common witchcraft terms quite frequently, including the following:

- Incantations and spells: Words (whether written, spoken, or thought) that are intentionally and carefully chosen to direct energy toward transforming yourself or a situation or system you are in.

- Intention: Your desired goal for a ritual and/or a guiding idea to carry with you before, during, and after the ritual. Intentions are often centered on a word/phrase/affirmation. For example, an intention might be something like the following: "May I interrupt unjust systems," or "May I find other disabled people to be in community with," or "May I direct what little strength I have today toward setting boundaries," etc. Intentions can be infused into any witchy ritual or tool, typically through visualization (directing your focus or energy toward an image in your mind that reflects your desired intention).

- Correspondences: Colors, textures, shapes, or other qualities that you and/or other witches associate with a desired trait, outcome, or intention in a situation (e.g., red for love, black for strength). In other words, correspondences are simply the magickal meanings you assign to anything: colors, textures, symbols, letters, words, tarot cards, etc. You can choose which items you use in your rituals based on these correspondences. I find there's magick in finding your own meaning for correspondences, but it can also be a great help to learn what other witches are doing. Friday Gladheart's *The Practical Witch's Almanac* includes many excellent resources about correspondences and other witchy terms.

How Is This Book Organized? And How Can You Use It?

This book is organized into nine chapters that include a total of 90 rituals centered on disability. Each chapter is focused on a different topic or theme, such as moon rituals, tarot, or relationships.

Because the rituals are arranged by topic, you can pick and choose what rituals you want to use when you want to use them, treating this book like a reference work. These are your rituals; they are up to your interpretation, and they invite you to adapt them for yourself, using the magick of being you. For instance, visualization is always an option if you aren't able to physically carry out all the steps of a ritual. Of if color correspondence isn't accessible to you visually, you can use other forms of correspondence instead, like texture or smell. In summary, bring your perspective and experiences to bear in what you choose to use, adapt, or discard.

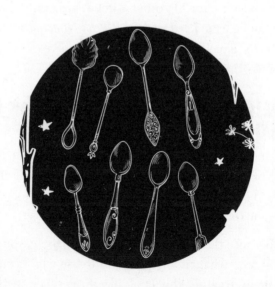

Chapter One: Rituals to Get You Started

No matter what your experience with the craft is, it can be daunting to add new rituals to your practice—let alone adding a whole focus, like disability in this case. Whether you're a brand-new witch or a seasoned practitioner, I wanted to open this book with rituals that will give you a good foundation to begin this journey. In this chapter, we'll cover making the craft your own (depending on your own experiences, values, and preferences), developing an ethical practice (with a special focus on avoiding cultural appropriation and other problematic bases for ritual), sourcing accessible tools, giving gratitude to your body and spoons, and combating the witchy imposter syndrome we may face as disabled people.

1. A Ritual for Making the Craft Your Own

The manifesto of this book is that witchcraft is for everyone. Everyone. I firmly believe this path is infinitely flexible and expansive. That means I believe the craft is available to people of any religion or no religion.

As a religious trauma survivor, I center my life on spiritual autonomy, and I seek to express that in the rituals I write. That's why I wrote this ritual. I wanted to create a ritual for beginning your craft on your terms: rejecting that which doesn't serve you, transforming the things that don't fit your life, and finding an undergirding sense of love and inclusion in your own practice—whether you call it spiritual or not. Basically, this ritual is about the witchcraft of spiritual autonomy and creativity. It's about making the craft your own.

[• • •]

What You'll Need for This Ritual:

- A candle (or safe and accessible equivalent) of a color that, to you, means "drawing in" or "attracting your intention"

Light the candle and say the following incantation.[4]

> *I am magick. I transform spaces of exclusion*
> *by my very presence as a disabled person. I*
> *claim the aspects of the craft that will lead*
> *to the inclusion of all of me and all other*
> *marginalized voices. I reject those parts of the*
> *craft that are based on ableist, sexist, racist,*
> *classist, homophobic, transphobic, or capitalist*
> *assumptions. I will transform the craft like all*
> *who have gone before and all who will come*

---

4 All incantations can either be spoken aloud, written out, or thought silently, depending on what works best for you.

after. I enter this conversation. I take up space.
This is my power.

Consider these questions:

- Do you consider yourself a spiritual or even religious person? Why or why not?

- What do these labels mean to you?

- What does witchcraft mean to you?

- What are your values when it comes to spiritual practice?

- As a disabled person, how have you been excluded from spiritual practices and spaces?

- How can you center your disabled experience in your craft, holding space for yourself and all the things that make you you—as you are?

- Through your craft, what do you want to transform in yourself and the world around you?

2. A Ritual for Developing Spoonie Craft Ethics

As a survivor of religious trauma, I always want to lay the groundwork for ethical engagement with spirituality. I love the Wiccan Rede as a baseline for this work; here is Lady Gwen Thompson's version: "An' it harm none, do what ye will."[5]

---

5 If you're interested in learning more about the history of this phrase, Patti Wigington's article "The Wiccan Rede" is an excellent place to start: https://www. learnreligions.com/the-wiccan-rede-2562601

For me, this means assessing (1) how the craft impacts me and (2) how the craft impacts others.[6] I put rituals, practices, and even beliefs through the following related questions.

Impacting Me

- Does this practice/ritual/belief help me take care of myself or fill me with a sense of shame or overwhelm?

- Is this practice/ritual/belief sustainable and accessible to me as a disabled person? Why or why not?

Impacting Others

- Does this practice/ritual/belief cause me to perpetuate unjust systems?

- Does this practice/ritual/belief deepen my understanding of others, or does it only reinforce my worldview or implicit biases?

After considering these questions, say the following incantation.

I seek to harm none and to work for a more just, inclusive, and magickal world for myself and others. As I enter into a new practice,

---

6 NOTE: As a white woman practicing witchcraft, I acknowledge that this space is fraught with cultural appropriation, usually committed by people like me (myself included). I know I have appropriated in ways I should not have and am committed to continuing to grow by centering the voices of practitioners of color. In the appendix in the back of this book, there is a list of resources on witchcraft and nature-based spiritual practice that center BIPOC voices.

belief, or ritual, I banish injustice of all kinds
and welcome in rituals that allow me to treat
myself and others with true love. I invoke this
power to learn, to listen when someone invites
me to a deeper understanding, to repair when I
do make mistakes, and to remain aware of my
own worth and power through it all—living
not in perfection but in the power of flexibility,
growth, and learning. This is my magick.

3. Lighting an Allergy-Friendly Candle

Picture this: You've just stepped into the local witchy shop. You're immediately in awe of the breadth of crystals, moons, oracle decks, and journals. But you're also immediately aware of your severe allergies. The incense is thick, and you can already feel the beginnings of a migraine. You also see a wall of multicolored candles, but their scent too is contributing to your migraine, even though you desperately would love to burn a candle in a ritual rooted in correspondences. What will you do?[7]

7 I realize this is a complicated issue, especially because local witchy shops are often community hubs that are operating on limited budgets and simply may not have the resources to provide the accommodations everyone needs. In fact, no individual space is going to be able to accommodate all disabilities and needs. In this case, I want to make an important note: incense can and does have so much spiritual meaning for so many people, and many people with disabilities different from mine might also feel very included in incense rituals. I share this detail not to shame the use of incense but to talk about my own experience with the complex world of disability inclusion and spiritual practices, and the ways I've found to participate with accommodations. If anything, this is an invitation to start the conversation, not end it, in the hopes that more and more spaces can exist that can accommodate various needs at various times for all witchy folks.

As an earth-loving, environmentally conscious human, I was heartbroken that I couldn't practice witchcraft with beautiful, ethically made candles of vibrant hues and perfumes.

I could afford neither the migraine nor the cost of candles like that. (Hello medical bills!)

It made me feel like an imposter.

Maybe you've felt the same way. Maybe you've been unable to enter a space or attend a spiritual gathering because it was inaccessible to people who use wheelchairs, have other mobility restrictions, are blind or low-vision, or have any number of other disabilities that I haven't listed or experienced myself. Maybe you've not been able to go to an event—or at least participate fully—because no sign language interpreter was available or accessible. In summary, regardless of your experience with disability—visible or invisible, accepted or dismissed—you've likely been excluded from rituals that otherwise called to you. And I want to hold space for that here.

In the case of the candles, I found my answer by letting go of perfection—accepting that disability accommodations are needed for me to exist and thus are necessary and beautiful as part of my spiritual practice.

My first step in accessing these accommodations was the dollar store. They had a number of battery-operated candles in various colors, and I decided this was a good start to adding candles to my practice.

It was exactly what I needed.

I went on to find battery-operated candles secondhand, choosing candles that could take rechargeable batteries. You can often find battery-operated candles at church rummage sales or buried in the home goods aisles of your local thrift store. You might even be able to find them at a yard sale.

Is this plastic-y solution perfect? No. But a huge part of sustainability is disability accommodation and monetary accessibility for all. And spirituality is no exception.

Of course, allergy-friendly solutions for candles will vary from person to person based on their individual allergies. Other options might include unscented candles or candles made of different materials than the ones that are setting off your particular allergies. Regardless, there is no shame in choosing the candle alternatives that work best for you and your health.

As you step into the following ritual, consider these questions:

- What aspects of witchcraft are inaccessible to you as a disabled person?

- What accommodations might be available to help you enter your desired practice?

- What lies might you be believing about your own worthiness of these accommodations?

- How might you rest in the love of all who care for you as you seek to find those accommodations?

Next, find a candle that is accessible, with attributes (like color or texture) that have a meaningful correspondence for you. If you're lighting a candle with a flame, find a clear, accessible space where it is safe to do so. Light or turn on the candle, then hold it or place it on a hard surface nearby.

Take a few deep breaths and repeat the following:

I am worthy of all disability accommodations I need in my spiritual craft. I call on the love of all who help me, and I take this power and turn it into resources. I give myself permission to transform the ordinary things around me into magick, to meet my needs and to connect to the divine, whatever that means for me. With this candle, I declare the sacredness of all practices that work for me. With this candle, I allow myself to meet my unique needs.

Blow out or turn off the candle. As the smoke (literal if you're using a flame candle, visualized metaphorically if you're using a battery-operated candle) rises, imagine the lies about unworthiness and disability accommodations floating away, disappearing, and being replaced by the candle of love and support. Carry this power with you throughout the day and always. Repeat as necessary to feel the power.

4. A Gratitude Ritual ... to Yourself and Your Spoons

If you're a disabled spoonie, you know it's so easy to get discouraged by the number of spoons you have in a day... and how quickly they disappear.

As I considered this reality in my own life, I wanted to create a ritual that honored the brave spoons that my body does give me, especially considering all it has to deal with. I wanted to honor that sacred line of spoons on my metaphorical table.

And so I used a little kitchen witchery, and I invite you to do so too.

A disclaimer: A ritual like this is not meant to promote toxic positivity or spiritual bypassing.

PsychologyToday.com defines toxic positivity as "the act of avoiding, suppressing, or rejecting negative emotions or experiences." And a part of toxic positivity is spiritual bypassing, which is "a tendency to use spiritual explanations to avoid complex psychological issues."[8]

As you may have gathered from the fiery, sweeping cussing, this is not a book for good vibes only. Shitty vibes and shitty days are part of the process and are regularly centered in my practice.

---

8 Gabriela Picciotto, Jesse Fox, and Félix Neto, "A phenomenology of spiritual bypass: Causes, consequences, and implications," J Spiritual Ment Health 20, no 4 (2018): 333–354, doi:10.1080/19349637.2017.1417756, as quoted in Kendra Cherry, MSEd, "Spiritual Bypassing as a Defense Mechanism," Verywell Mind, March 17, 2023, https://www.verywellmind.com/what-is-spiritual-bypassing-5081640.

Gratitude is about honoring what is, not sweeping it away. And that's what this ritual will focus on.

[• • •]

What You'll Need for This Ritual:

- Literal spoons from your kitchen (these can also simply be visualized if necessary)

- A table or other flat surface

Before you begin this ritual, consider the following questions:

- What things in your life take up the most spoons?

- Are there ways you could limit those things through accommodations or other support?

- What things replenish your energy? How can you invite those things to be more a part of your life?

- What energy-giving things—big or small—can you bring into your life? What energy-draining things can you remove from your life?

Next, perform or visualize the following things:

Gather the available literal spoons in your house. Lay them out on the table in a line (or some other meaningful and accessible shape). Count them. Then go down the line or around the shape and say the following to each spoon:

I honor your existence. I thank you for the
energy you provide.

Then, pick the spoon up and hold it to your heart, saying
the following:

I will listen to my body. I reject those things that
are not necessary and that drain my energy. I
invite those things that replenish me, honoring
the spoons within me, the spoons that I have
here.

5. Reminder Ritual: You Are (Witchy) Enough

In the beautiful, expansive world of witchcraft and
spirituality in general, it's so easy to compare ourselves
to others. As disabled people, we have the added burden
of accessibility issues, the possibility of low spoonage,
and a range of accommodation needs that may or may not
be met by our communities, or that we may not be able
to meet due to lack of any kind of resources (especially
budget resources—ugh, capitalism).

Let me assure you: no matter your spoons, no matter
your diagnoses (or lack thereof), no matter your experience,
no matter your religious background (or lack thereof), no
matter what-have-you, you are witchy enough. In fact, your
individual background is necessary and brings a unique
magick, an unexpected alchemy to the cosmic community.
So, light a candle or accessible alternative of your choice,
and repeat after me:

If this path calls to me, I am witchy.

I am connected to nature.

I am connected to love.

I bring my own magickal fingerprints to my existence.

I bring my own disabled experience to my resistance.

I am witchy enough.

Chapter Two: Moon Rituals

Like many witches, I am in love with the moon and integrate it strongly into my practices. One of my favorite aspects of the moon, in the context of disability, is that the moon itself is something that hovers over and includes all of us. None of us are completely cut off from it. As disabled witches, while our different disabilities may cause us to interact with the moon in different ways, it is ultimately accessible and for us all.

With this in mind, the rituals in this chapter will explore how the moon phases invite us into distinctly disabled witchcraft, with a special emphasis on the spoonie lens of disability. We will walk through the broad phases of the moon and the ways we can invite that rhythm into our own unique practices through adaptable rituals. Personally, I really appreciate the way Kalia Kelmenson describes the meanings of the moon phases in her September 2023 article "The Spiritual Meaning of Moon Phases," published by *Spirituality & Health*, which I will reference throughout this section.

6. Moon Phases, Spoon Phases

As both a witch and a spoonie, I find much meaning in the moon. I wrote about this at *All The Threads*, my Substack newsletter:

The moon goes in phases, and my symptoms—mental, physical, and everything in between—go in phases. On days when it's bad, I remember that the brightness of a metaphorical full moon is on the rise. On days when it's good, I remember the importance of the darkness of periods of rest. On the really bad days, I remember that eclipses don't last forever . . . in a day, in a week, in a month, or maybe even in a year, things will feel better again. Through it all, the moon is still the beloved moon . . . and I am still the beloved me.

If you're a witch with moon-based practices, consider how those phases relate to your own disabled experience. If you have special moon rituals, maybe you could add an incantation like the one below:

Today is [insert phase].

Like the moon, I am complete,

regardless of the phases of my spoons,

regardless of the way I am perceived by an ableist society.

The moon's magick is available to me today and always.

I call upon the power of [insert phase] to help me bring my intentions into being.

7. New Moon Ritual for Spoonies

What does the new moon phase mean to you? Kelmenson writes that the new moon is "a time of pause."

As spoonies, we are no stranger to pause. In fact, we must rest more than non-disabled people do.

All humans need rest, but our capitalist world refuses to acknowledge that. Even non-disabled people, who have more resources to comply with this system, feel forced to do so. But our disability magickally disrupts that system. We don't have the option not to rest, and frankly, neither do non-disabled people (they just can hide it better). Therefore, we are uniquely positioned to align with the natural phases of the moon and our bodies.

Next time you observe a new moon, take stock of how your body is feeling. Ask yourself these questions:

- In what ways do you need to rest right now?

- How might you change your routines to better align with how your body requests rest?

If you have the opportunity, sit beneath the new moon in a safe and accessible location (even if it's just by a window in your residence). Breathe in the compassion of this phase, even under the cloak of night. Receive this care like a blanket or some other comfort item that makes you feel loved and connected. Once you are relaxed, consider and repeat this intention:

I am worthy of rest. New moon, remind me of
this. I rest in this phase and my power. I am
enough.

8. Waxing Moon Ritual for Spoonies

What do the waxing moon phases[9] mean to you?
Kelmenson writes that the waxing moon calls us to "get
in motion."

In an ableist society, there is sometimes this narrative
that disabled people can do nothing. That we are simply
unwanted burdens, incapable of having dreams or
achieving any of our goals.

While we certainly need accommodations, disabled
people are human too—with goals, dreams, and hopes. The
waxing moon invites us to live into that power. We have
fewer spoons than most (and often more obstacles), so we
are especially qualified to prioritize the dreams and goals
we have for ourselves and our communities.

Next time you observe a waxing moon, take stock of
your goals by reflecting on these questions:

- In what ways do you want to put your power into
  motion?

- What accommodations are in place, or could be put
  in place, to allow you to reach your goals?

---

9 For simplicity, I am including all waxing moon phases here—from crescent to
gibbous—since the waxing of the moon is a gradual process over multiple days.

- What are goals that you authentically want and that are within reach? What are three small steps you can take on this magickal journey of transformation and harnessing your own resources and power?

If you have the opportunity, sit beneath the waxing moon in a safe and accessible location (even if it's just by a window in your residence). Breathe in the light of this phase, even though it is only partial. Once you are relaxed, consider and repeat this intention:

I am worthy of goals and dreams, capable of making things happen with a keen and magickal sense of prioritization brought about by my awareness of my own resources as a disabled person. Waxing moon, remind me of this reality. I rest in this phase and my power. I am magick.

9. Full Moon Ritual for Spoonies

What does the full moon phase mean to you? Kelmenson writes that the full moon, with its "radiant glory" as "the showiest of the phases," calls us to "savor [our] life."

As a disabled person, I often feel a narrative weighing on me: that I am not a whole person because of my disabilities. While I certainly have challenges and need accommodations, my wholeness as a human is in no way diminished by my diagnosis and experience. Quite the contrary: those experiences are a part of the identity that makes me whole.

The full moon invites us to live into that magickal reality. We are whole, complete, and expansive. In this phase, we declare, craters and all, that we are magnificent and powerful, like the moon.

Next time you observe a full moon, ask yourself these questions:

- In what ways do you feel whole?

- In what ways do you not feel whole?

- How do ableist expectations play into these feelings?

- How can you show up as your full and authentic self, expressing yourself and your full experience, even in situations where your disabilities may take up more space than is considered polite in ableist society?

If you have the opportunity, sit beneath the full moon in a safe and accessible location (even if it's just by a window in your residence). Breathe in the light of this phase, feeling how it unflinchingly takes up space. Once you are relaxed, consider and repeat this intention:

I take up space, like the full moon, for I too am whole and magnificent. Full moon, remind me of this truth. I rest in this phase and my power

to subvert expectations by my very presence, to
exert change and transformation just by being
myself. I am magick, just like the full moon.

10. Waning Moon Ritual for Spoonies

What do the waning moon phases[10] mean to you? Kelmenson writes that the waning moon encourages a "letting go."

Sometimes, ableist expectations can become a very practical reality and hindrance in our lives, especially when it comes to our very real to-do lists.

As spoonies, we know the importance of allocating our spoons with wisdom and respect for our bodies' rhythms, and the waning moon invites us to do just that.

If the moon can release or "let go," can't we also let go, as powerful, magickal beings underneath the moon's love?

Next time you observe a waning moon, consider what your daily to-do list looks like. Ask yourself these questions:

- What is on your to-do list?

- What things on this list do you want and need to do?

- What things on this list are expectations but are not essential or are not aligned with your goals, wants, needs, or spoons?

10 For simplicity, I am including all waning moon phases here—from gibbous to crescent—since the waning of the moon is a gradual process over multiple days.

- What accommodations are in place, or could be put in place, to allow you to do the tasks you need to do and let go of the expectations that do not serve?

If you have the opportunity, sit beneath the waning moon in a safe and accessible location (even if it's just by a window in your residence). Breathe in the light of this phase, even though it fades. Once you are relaxed, consider and repeat this intention:

> *I honor this phase of waning—and, with it, my*
> *waning spoons—by letting go of expectations*
> *and tasks that do not serve. Waning moon,*
> *remind me of this freedom. I rest in this phase*
> *and my power to make decisions and transform*
> *my to-do list from ableist to disabled witchcraft.*
> *I am magick, by the light of the waning moon.*

Chapter Three: Nature Rituals

*A*s witches, one of the most central parts of our practice is nature. In it, we find connection to the divine (however we understand it) and all of the universe. But to be disabled in a capitalist hellscape means not always having access to participation in nature-based rituals.

In the rituals in this chapter, I'll talk about some of the ways I have faced inaccessible natural spaces and how I found ways to express my witchy spirituality. It's my hope that the rituals in this chapter will create space for you to participate with nature in ways that work for you, even as you use and adapt these rituals as needed for your own disabilities.

11. Finding Nature Items When You Have Allergies

Picture this. You're an aspiring green witch, but all the green witchery books have one thing in common: they suggest using things you're allergic to.

I speak from experience. I'm an eclectic witch[11] with a lot of love for the green witch path, but my severe allergies take traditional foraging for my rituals off the table.

Many of you are in the same boat. Maybe you've been told you're not a real green witch if you can't forage, if

---

11 Eclectic witches are witches that don't follow one particular path of witchcraft/ spirituality.

you don't have access to certain plants, if your tiny but sort of affordable apartment can't sustain the gorgeous, gigantic foraged altars of Instagram, if the nearest nature trails are not accessible to you due to disability or any other reason, etc.

But access isn't what makes a witch. Intention is.

Connection to the earth is not a privilege for the non-disabled few. It's the birthright of all humans—indeed all living things—upon this wonderful, stardusty planet.

So what does intention with nature rituals look like if you're disabled?

I developed this ritual to answer that. The first step is to consider the following question: What nature-based practices or rituals do you want to participate in but have been barred from?

Once you have that answer, develop a forager mindset for the resources you already have.

If you're looking for specific nature items . . .

- Do you have something around the house that could represent them?

- Could you draw the plants in a notebook you have lying around?

- Could you find a picture online of the desired item and print it off at the library . . . or even pull it up on your device's screen while you perform the ritual?

- Is there a mental visualization you could use to represent these items?

- Are audio or written guided meditations related to these items available online?

- Could a miniature model of this be found in the toy section of the thrift store or in a Buy Nothing group?

- Could you substitute one of the desired items with an inexpensive and comparable spice from your grocery store aisle?

This is by no means an exhaustive list of questions. Trust your own creativity and ingenuity. I believe in you.

Because here's the thing. Disabled people are amazing foragers. We're scrappy and have to piece together medical teams, remedies, conflicting and interacting diagnoses, insurance, HSA accounts, bargaining with billing offices, switching providers, complex schedules and changing factors affecting our spoons for the day, accessible transportation, etc.

Why should green witchery be off limits when disabled people are *this* good at foraging?

So, once you've gathered the substitute items for your desired ritual(s), you can infuse your foraged finds with this intention.

I gathered abundance where there was none.

*I transformed items from nature with my
disabled ingenuity.*

My creativity is magick.

I consecrate these items as sacred.

*I invoke the power they have just by existing in
this world,*

Made of the same stardust as me.

My power is enough.

12. Earth Incantation to Honor Your Body

Many witches center their rituals around the four elements: earth, water, air, and fire. I'm no different in my practice. The next few rituals, then, will be element-centered incantations related to disability.

The first is an earth incantation.

As a disabled person, you may have a fraught relationship with earth. You may have been told you don't belong here or that you're such an aberration that you don't deserve the stardust that makes you up. Maybe you've even been implicitly or explicitly barred from your favorite parts of the earth because of accessibility issues.

Rest assured that even if you've been estranged from earth, the earth has not estranged herself/himself/itself/themselves/[insert any pronoun you associate with the earth] from you. You are a beloved, invaluable, earthy, stardusty being of sacred light and power.

I'm no stranger to being estranged from earth. Growing up in a religiously traumatic environment, I was taught that the world was spiritually evil. And one of my most prominent disabilities is my severe allergies to most types of trees, pollen, and creatures—allergies that cause debilitating, multi-day migraines. In short, my body has been forced to be at war with the earth, and I am seeking to repair that relationship. And it's rituals like the below that have been instrumental on that healing path.

May this ritual help you on that journey too. May you find in earth a friend more inclusive, more celebratory, more untamed than capitalism and ableism. May you know that your war with earth is over.

Before you begin this earth-centered incantation, take a moment to ponder the earth, using these guided questions if they call to you:

- How does the ground feel beneath you? If you're not able to feel the ground beneath you, how about another grounding surface that you can touch?

- What is your favorite place on the earth? What do you like about that place? How does it make you feel?

- As a disabled person, here on the earth, where do you feel alienated or marginalized?

- The earth and everything on it is ultimately made of stardust. What does this unity mean to you?

At this point, you may want to express any feelings, images, or associations you have with these or other reflection questions. It can be very magickal to express these thoughts in a creative way—infused with the intention of finding connection with the earth. A few possible options include journaling, drawing, sewing, knitting, painting, interpretive dance, and singing, listening to, or engaging with a resonant song.

Next, visualize yourself as stardust, as part of the earth. Sit with the idea that you are held in all the love of all that is and was on the earth. Rest in the idea that you are a worthy part of it all.

Think of the ways you've been asked to take up less space as a disabled person. Now think of how big the earth is.

You are never too much.

Stretch yourself as wide as you can, keeping your feet planted on the earth below. If you're not able to do this, stretch out another part of your body, or simply visualize yourself being stretched wide and connected to the earth.

When you feel ready, repeat the following incantation three times:

Like earth, I am made of stardust. I am
magickal. I am connected to the universe, to
all who have gone before, to all who will come
after. My body is enough and magnificent and

disabled all at the same time. I declare this body
honored, beloved, whole, sacred. I declare this
body worthy of care and attention and rest and
joy and all emotions. I carry this power with
me always, from this day forward, past, present,
and future.

13. Water Incantation to Honor the Cycle of You

The second of our element-centered, disability-focused incantations is about water.

As a disabled person and witchy spoonie, I've always felt most seen in one central aspect of witchcraft: the cyclical nature of it. And what is more cyclical than the waves?

Sometimes ferocious, sometimes calm. Sometimes powerfully and loudly expanding their beauty over the beachy land, sometimes receding into the distance behind boundaries. What a metaphor for disability! We can express powerfully, distantly, expansively, quietly, and loudly. It's a testament to our resilience and adaptability, as well as the paradoxical boxes we're expected to fit into in an ableist world.

Be sick, but not too sick. Look sick, but only when it is convenient to the system. Be anything but your own experience, which is just too expansive to accept.

Fuck it. You are waves. You are water. Don't let anyone diminish the sea that is you.

Because the world needs the tides, just like the world needs the voices of the disabled community. Like water, disability can have disruptive effects, but that disruption is transformative and pushes against ableist structures. Your body's power will transform, however slowly, the system that capitalism wants: work-work-work, do-don't-be. In a word, your watery, disabled body is magick.

For this ritual, consider going to be near a body of water, if that is safe and accessible to you. Another alternative is to take a bath or shower. Or you can simply visualize yourself with the water.

Before you begin this water-centered incantation, take a moment to ponder water, using these guided questions if they call to you:

- How does water feel against your skin?

- As a disabled person, how does the cycle of waves remind you of your own experiences?

- What is your favorite body of water? What do you like about that place? How does it make you feel?

- All human beings need water, and the tides are a part of all of our experiences. What does this unity mean to you?

Dip your hand or toe in the water (or visualize yourself doing so). Repeat the following incantation when you are ready:

O water, I am united to you and all life through you. I too am like the waves—expansive and boundaried, strong and calm, ferocious and beautiful. I claim my power to name my needs, to exist in ways that are natural but demonized, to transform ableist structures just by existing. I am like water. Though my transformative work may be gradual, it WILL take effect.

14. Air Incantation to Honor Your Breath

Our next element-centered, disability-focused incantation is about air.

If you're a disabled person with a history of trauma (which I'm guessing is most of you reading right now), you know the importance of breathwork—the use of breath to ground yourself. But, if you're like me, you might be a perfectionist about breathwork. That's why I created this incantation.

My often-severe allergies make breathwork challenging, because my access to breathing through my nose or mouth isn't always quite as free. As a religious trauma survivor with PTSD, I also find some breathwork meditation exercises triggering due to their association with some spiritually abusive and severely perfectionistic environments I've dealt with. And this doesn't even acknowledge the experience of disabled people with other more direct breathing challenges, including asthma and many others.

What it comes down to is this: we as disabled people often face inaccessibility even when it comes to the most basic of needs (and elements). In this case, with air, we sometimes have to be creative to breathe meditatively or for grounding and stress relief.

But here's the thing: no matter what accessibility issues stand in your way, you're already an expert at breathing. You've been breathing, surviving, inhaling, exhaling through pain, misdiagnoses, invasive medical procedures, gaslighting, bullying, ableist systems. Your lungs are amazing, even if they've had to suffer under oppression and even if they need significant medical assistance. Your very breath is magick defiance.

You are magick.

If you're interested in more accessible breathwork exercises, listen to your body, reach out to medical practitioners on your team, and read various experts on the subject.[12] And if breathwork itself is not connecting with you, that's okay.

However you interact with breath, this incantation will remind you that air is yours.

Before you begin, take a moment to ponder air, using these guided questions if they call to you:

• How does wind feel against your skin?

---

12 Dr. Faith G. Harper's Unfuck Your Body is a great place to start.

- As a disabled person, how does the process of inhaling and exhaling remind you of your own experiences?

- Where do you feel you can breathe the easiest? Why?

- All human beings breathe. What does this unity mean to you?

Now repeat the following incantation:

> *I deserve to be here. I take in breath and exhale it out, according to the rhythms of my magickal body. I inhale the truths of my own worthiness and power. I exhale unjust systems, with the power of my very breath. With each breath, I transform myself, existing. With each breath, I transform the world around me, to receive me.*

15. Fire Incantation to Honor Your Fight Against Unjust Systems

We've covered incantations about the first three elements commonly used in witchcraft: earth, water, and air. Now we move on to the fourth and final element: fire.

In keeping with the theme of resistance and disability, I can think of no more evocative image than fire. Fire is disruptive, intense, powerful, and apt to cause transformation. Disability is much the same.

If you have low spoons, that torches through capitalistic expectations. If you need mobility accommodations, that torches through ableist building assumptions. If you need medication to live, that torches through money-hungry billionaires' belief that healthcare isn't a goddamn human right.

So, bright flame, your very magickal body is a fiery form of resistance. And that's what this incantation is about.

Before you begin this fire-centered incantation, take a moment to ponder fire, using these guided questions if they call to you:

- How does the warmth of a candle, fireplace, or bonfire feel to you?[13]

- As a disabled person, what qualities of fire remind you of your own experiences?

- In what spaces do you feel most empowered to use your fiery voice to resist? Why?

- Fire is a universal human experience, with the warmth it provides, the power it exudes, and the disruption it can cause. What does this unity mean to you?

Now repeat the following incantation:

---

13 As a person with severe allergies, it's hard for me to be around traditional candles and even bonfires, so I use LED candles. Answer this question in accordance with any accommodations you need.

Like a forest fire declaring that climate change is real, my fiery, disabled existence is resistance. My fiery voice is needed and deserves to be heard. I call on this power to resist in whatever ways are possible for me. I invoke the power of fire to torch unjust systems.

16. Love Spell: Resting in the Rooted Love of Trees

Often, witches are asked to perform love spells (usually for sexual or romantic love), and these spells are often misunderstood as taking the place of true connection and relationship work.

But as disabled people, we know the power of a resourcing community as an expression of love, and we also know that quick fixes for connection (romantic and otherwise) don't work.

And as witchy spoonies, we have a source of love to draw from: trees. Trees actually take care of their communities. According to some ecologists, "trees are 'social creatures' that communicate with each other in cooperative ways." They "are linked to neighboring trees by an underground network of fungi that resembles the neural networks in the brain," sharing resources and important information with each other.[14]

---

14 Dave Davies, "Trees Talk to Each Other. 'Mother Tree' Ecologist Hears Lessons for People, Too," May 4, 2021, NPR, https://www.npr.org/sections/health-shots/2021/05/04/993430007/trees-talk-to-each-other-mother-tree-ecologist-hears-lessons-for-people-too>.

Undergirding witchcraft is a deep respect for the connection we all share with nature, and I can think of few more beautiful examples of that connection than what the trees do to help each other.

That's why I wrote this love spell—to draw on that love of nature within witchcraft and to challenge the outside expectation that we can create instant love connections without any personal work on the part of the person requesting the love spell. A tree love spell declares what disabled people already know: love isn't about instant gratification but about showing up through it all in honesty, authenticity, kindness, repair, and readjustments.

The disabled community is about sharing resources, a kind of tree love. And when we are feeling like our community is lacking, we can look to trees as a baseline— we have the love of trees and all who have gone before and will come after. We are connected.

[• • •]

What You'll Need for This Ritual:

- Optional: a crystal, candle, or other magickal item of your choice with a correspondence of love

- A tree to sit near or an accessible item or location that will help you visualize trees

Visualize trees or go to a physical location with a tree you can be next to in whatever way is comfortable for you, holding, bringing along, or visualizing any items you associate with correspondences of love. Visualize yourself being surrounded by love in the shape of the roots, branches, and trunk. Connect to the feel of the tree on your back or its roots underneath you. Imagine the networks that connect this tree to other trees and also to you.

Repeat the following:

> *Oh trees, I invoke your love for me and all of nature. I invoke your connection. I invoke this sense of love and connection through all my doings. Fill me with your sense of care. I thank you for your love. I thank you for your magick.*

17. When You Feel Like Goo: Channeling Butterfly Energy

We've all seen inspirational quotes and posters about the transformation of caterpillar into butterfly. It's absolutely cliché at this point, though still absolutely wondrous.

But the less wondrous bit of this whole process is the goo part; in an article for *Scientific American*, Ferris Jabr explains: "the caterpillar digests itself, releasing enzymes to dissolve all of its tissues" so that "if you were to cut open a cocoon or chrysalis at just the right time, caterpillar soup would ooze out."

This whole process really reminds me of the bad spoon days of the disabled life—days when self-care is so basic that to capitalist society it looks like we are doing "nothing."

Our magick is in the resistance to these norms. Our bodies declare that the quiet transformation of goo days is not only valid but necessary. No goo, no butterfly. No rest, no acknowledgment of humanity.

And thus, by resting on the days we feel spoonless and gooey, we are transforming ableist systems by interrupting them, wrapped in our cocoon of rebirth and rejuvenation, whatever that healing rest looks like for us and our own bodies' rhythms.

So on those days when nothing but rest gets done, visualize the transformation of the butterfly—especially the goo part—repeating the following:

> *In rest on my zero-to-low-spoon days, I channel the energy of the transforming butterfly. I feel like a soup of my own needs, and that is what I need today for the transformative power of my magick. I am enough and powerful and magickal through all my phases. This is my power.*

Chapter Four: A Disabled Wheel of the Year

The Wheel of the Year is central to the practice of many modern witches because of the way these holidays connect directly to the cycles of the earth. However, as with other pieces of witchy practice, we as disabled people can at times be kept out of celebrations and rituals because of accessibility issues. In this chapter, we'll look at a spoonie ritual for low-spoon holidays, as well as a complete walkthrough of the Wheel of the Year from a disabled perspective.

18. Using the Wheel of the Year When You Can't Be Present: When Your Spoons Don't Match the Season

Like many witches, I adore the Wheel of the Year. As a severe-allergy spoonie, it's one of a few ways I can actually connect to nature. But therein lies the problem. Sometimes my body's rhythms don't match the seasons.

For example, Litha is a time of celebration, but on Litha 2023, during the time I was writing this book, I was dealing with a severe, incredibly painful weeks-long interstitial cystitis flare, as well as some painful, abusive situations.

I remember lying down on my back and exhaling loudly, willing my sunflower-shaped earrings to put me in the summer solstice mood. But I didn't feel like celebrating Litha. Was I a bad witch?

Maybe you've felt the same way.

Let me assure you that you are not a bad witch for being disabled. As I've said before, disability is itself a form of transformative magick of resistance to an ableist system.

So before we move on to the rituals for the Wheel of Year, let's begin with an incantation for the times when the spiritual rituals don't fit.[15]

> *Today is _____ (insert witchy holiday).*
>
> *I feel _____.*
>
> *It is enough.*
>
> *I am magick as I am.*
>
> *I take the correspondences, meanings, and magick of this day and transform them toward inclusion, for this too is magick.*
>
> *This ritual, this day, this festival is bigger than ableist expectations.*
>
> *I call upon my power to transform and transmute where this is needed.*

---

15 As a queer exvangelical, I'm no stranger to contending with, and often reimagining, rituals that don't fucking fit me.

I rest upon the love of all who have gone before,
who are here now, and who will come after.

I belong here too.

There is space for me.

I can celebrate or not celebrate the way I need
to.

This is magick.

I am magick.

19. Wheel of the Year: A Samhain Ritual Centered on Disability

Like many witches, I find my favorite witchy holiday to be Samhain. I've always adored Halloween, so this is fitting. Fall is very important to me spiritually: I was born in the fall, I met my long-term partner in the fall, and I have always adored the changing of the leaves, the decorating of pumpkins, the crisp air in my part of the world, and the celebration of Halloween.

So you can imagine my joy when at the beginning of my witchy journey, I discovered that Samhain is considered to be a time of "celebrating the Witches' New Year" (which is why we're starting this disabled Wheel of the Year journey here), with an emphasis on "the cycle of death and rebirth" and "reconnect[ing] with our ancestors" in this "time when the veil between our world and the spirit realm is thin."[16] Because of my experience with fall, it was already a reflective time, so I felt incredibly validated by the Wheel of the Year in this case.

With all that in mind, one popular ritual for this time of year is to include your ancestors in your altar space in some way, often with a lit candle or other things associated with them. And I want to note here that I don't consider ancestors to be limited to blood relations. For any number of reasons, found family often provides just as much community and connection as legal and/or biological family—if not more and in a healthier way, in some cases. (See ritual #70 for more on found family.) And here's the thing: we're all made of stardust; everyone and everything is, in some way, our ancestors. Our connection to all of nature is so important to witchiness, and an expansive understanding of our ancestors is a part of that.

And while you certainly can spend lots of money on making an ancestor-centered altar, you don't have to. You can use pictures you already have of your chosen ancestors, as well as candles or other objects or accessible alternatives that you already own.

That's the beauty of the mystery of this time of year (and the whole Wheel of the Year): it's not about what you use but the intention you infuse it with. Connecting with the ancestors—the beloved dead, all who came before

16 Patti Wigington, "All About Samhain," Learn Religions, July 10, 2019, https://www.learnreligions.com/all-about-samhain-2562691.

and will come after, in whatever way we conceive of them—also allows us to take stock of the past year with an undergirding sense of love and support. With this in mind, take this incantation and make it your own:

In this new year of change, death, rebirth, I reinvent myself again, existing and resisting with intention. With a thin veil in mind, I focus my energy on the love of my chosen ancestors and beloved dead as I seek to pursue these intentions. I ask for my ancestors' help in releasing any intentions that would not serve me or are not rooted in care for myself and others, even as I honor and remember the ways they lived with intention and resistance. This is the magick of Samhain, and this is my power.

20. Wheel of the Year: A Yule Ritual Centered on Disability

Yule is the celebration of the winter solstice, and this is a day of great celebration for me as a severe-allergy spoonie, as it marks the time of year when I can be outside more regularly (bundled up of course). It's a time of quiet, of rest, of cold.

It's also dark and a bit treacherous travel-wise. As I've mentioned before when discussing the Wheel of the Year, it's okay if you have dichotomous emotions and experiences with these days, especially as a disabled person. For me, Yule is especially dichotomous because it falls near Christmas, an important holiday to my Christian faith, which was weaponized against me (and any person who wasn't a Christian or even a "good enough" Christian) during my time growing up in conservative white evangelical fundamentalism.

To hold space for all of these tensions and to reclaim this time as one of resistance as a disabled and queer and witchy person, I wrote the following to repeat at Yule, coinciding with the themes of the Advent candles (which are Christian but were somewhat forbidden in my anti-Catholic growing-up environment). It is an incantation that is open to all.

[• • •]

What You'll Need for This Ritual:

- Four candles (or accessible alternative)

Read the following incantation, aloud or silently, lighting a candle at each stanza:

Hope: Earth

Light a candle for hope.

We are all made of earth, of stars.

May this give us hope for solidarity.

Peace: Air

Light a candle for peace.

We all breathe in, breathe out.

May this give us peace enough to hold space for each other.

Joy: Water

Light a candle for joy.

We all splash and play in oceans, lakes, rivers, ponds.

May this give us joy to resist together the crush of oppression.

Love: Fire

Light a candle for love.

We all are entranced, destroyed, mobilized, reborn by fire.

May this blaze of love lead to justice for all.

21. Wheel of the Year: An Imbolc Ritual Centered on Disability

Imbolc takes place in early February, with a focus on new beginnings. It is the midpoint between a solstice and an equinox, and in my hemisphere, that means that the days start getting longer. It is a celebration of spring and hope.

As disabled people, we need a lot of hope: hope that we will find the resources to fill in the gaps of accommodations, hope that our communities will fight alongside us for our rights. For me, Imbolc is an invitation to lean into that hope, into that reminder of transformation. The barrenness of winter is over, and spring is on the way. Our existence functions like a spring morning over a barren ableist capitalist hellscape. In bleak times of limited accommodations and terrible policies, we can hold on to hope that our resistance is not in vain.

[• • •]

What You'll Need for This Ritual:

- Some items or ideas that mean spring/hope to you

- Some items or ideas that mean winter/difficulty to you

- A candle (or safe and accessible equivalent)

- A flat surface on which you can place all the items

Light the candle. Arrange or visualize the items that mean spring to you on one side of your candle. Arrange or visualize the items that mean winter to you on the other side of the candle. Now, connect the two sides to form a circle around the candle (or visualize the same) and repeat the following incantation.

> *Imbolc is here. A sign of hope and increased light. I set my intentions for springtime to fall on [desired cause, accommodations, etc.]. I invoke this power. I am magick during all the seasons of the year and of my body.*

22. Wheel of the Year: An Ostara Ritual Centered on Disability

I've always adored the word *equinox*, long before I was formally practicing witchcraft. The name just sounds mysterious and magickal.

And there is something so hope-inspiring about the spring equinox, which is what Ostara commemorates on the Wheel of the Year (in my hemisphere). Rebirth has been an important idea to me in both of my spiritual paths (Christian and witch).

It's also been an important idea to me as a disabled person. In the ever-changing landscape of symptoms, diagnoses, treatments, and spoon levels, I am constantly reinventing myself, ever connected to the resourceful and abundant energy that permeates spring. I find myself again and again, helping each iteration find what abundance looks like for her.

My survival has depended on this ability to be reborn amidst the ableist society I live in. I'm an unwanted and scrappy wildflower on the overly manicured lawns of suburbia. I've survived winters, and I continue to pop back up from the apparent grave of low-spoon seasons. If that doesn't scream spring and Ostara energy, I don't know what does.

Spoonies are resurrection experts. And that's why I wrote this ritual.

[• • •]

What You'll Need for This Ritual:

- A seed of your choice
- A journal/grimoire (or otherwise available equivalent)

Before you embark on this ritual, consider the following questions:

- What does spring mean to you? How are your spoon levels during spring?
- What parts of spring celebrations in our society are you barred from?

- How can you reclaim and rebirth those celebrations, transforming them from ableist to wildly inclusive?

If you can, write your answers in your journal or grimoire. Then hold the seed, visualizing an intention of rebirth coming from within you. Finally, say the following incantation:

> *Like a seed, I may not look like there is rebirth in me. And yet within the seed, and within me, is great power. This Ostara, I invoke that renewing power within myself and from the love of all who have gone before, my current community, and those who will come after.*
> *I transform ableist spaces with my presence, growing, changing, dying, rebirthing. I rise like a seedling, strong and nurtured by the earth. My body holds the magick of Ostara.*

23. Wheel of the Year: A Beltane Ritual Centered on Disability

When I think of Beltane (May Day), I think of one witchy practice: the maypole. I've never participated in a group maypole before for a number of accessibility reasons, including one in particular: my severe allergies limit my outside time significantly, and May is a really bad allergy time, threatening to bring on multi-day migraines and/or severely painful and long-lasting interstitial cystitis flares.

But that doesn't mean maypoles can't be transformed into an accessible ritual, even from the comfort of your own home during a fucking flare or some other accessibility issue. Below is one possibility for a maypole ritual. This ritual involves movement, music, and constructing a mini maypole, but remember that you can always adapt these rituals to your own accessibility needs (for example, by leaving out the music or by using visualization in place of physical movement).

[• • •]

What You'll Need for This Ritual:

- A space in your home where you are free to move or visualize in a way that feels good

- Ribbons or anything similar that is available to you; make sure they are all of similar lengths

- A stick or similar item

- Some kind of adhesive (tape, glue, etc.)

- A device for playing music (like a phone)

Adhere the ribbons to the top of the stick to construct a mini maypole.

Once your mini maypole is complete, turn on your favorite songs. Then, if possible, lift the pole up in the air and spin or move it (and even yourself) in whatever way feels comfortable to you, allowing the ribbons to dramatically wrap around the mini pole. Dance (or otherwise engage with the music in a way that is accessible for you) for however long feels good to you, then complete the ritual with this incantation:

Today, I celebrate Beltane, transforming items
from my home into a maypole. I am worthy
of taking up space, of existing in celebratory
rituals, spoons or no spoons. I invoke this
Beltane power by my own transformative dance,
for I am magick.

Other Beltane Activities

Creating your own mini maypole isn't the only accessible way to celebrate Beltane. Another option is to have an indoor maypole celebration. Gather like-minded friends and set up a pole that you can dance around (or otherwise engage with, with or without music) together in the traditional fashion, just inside and with any accommodations you may need.

I could also see another alternative. I'm a spoonie who occasionally does pole dancing at a local gym. It might be possible to rent out a practice room at a similar gym for an accessible indoor maypole gathering for Beltane, making any necessary accommodations.

And finally, let's not forget that Beltane is associated with fertility and sex. Sexual celebration rituals are for ALL who want them, as long as they are done in a safe and consensual way. If this is something you want to engage with, consider taking some sexual self-care time for yourself and/or with one or more partners. Be safe and have fun. If this sounds good to you, remember that you are worth it, whatever sex looks like for you.[17]

24. Wheel of the Year: A Litha Ritual Centered on Disability

Litha, the witchy celebration of the summer solstice, is just that . . . a celebration. But that light celebratory vibe doesn't always match my spoon levels. Summer is a bad symptom time for me—my allergies worsen, the heat and air quality negatively impact my symptoms, and summer is associated with some painful memories that sometimes kick up additional mental health symptoms.

Still, summer does give me a sense of hope. There's something magickal about growing sunflowers, lightning bugs, visiting the beach, wildflowers, and the brightness of the sun. All of these do scream joy and wonder.

Maybe you have a similar experience. Rest assured, Litha is for us, even in our complex and sometimes conflicting experience of joy.

To me, as a disabled witch, Litha is an opportunity to focus on two ideas: (1) the joy I have at my own uniqueness and (2) the promise of days when spoons are more plentiful. Litha is a celebration of the full human experience and, indeed, the full disabled experience. I am more than low-spoon days. I am more than painful treatments and complex

17 For an incantation you can use before sex, see ritual #68.

logistical questions. I am more than the diagnoses that label me. I am me.

For me, Litha is a defiant commemoration of the resistance of disabled joy.

This Litha ritual will involve whatever means joy to you. Put on your favorite outfit, turn on joyful music. Maybe dance, maybe simply sway, move in whatever way feels good to your body. Or work on a creative hobby you enjoy expressing yourself with. Or call up friends and enjoy the music together or watch movies or shows that fill you with joy.

Conclude this celebratory ritual with the following words, lighting a candle (or accessible equivalent) with a correspondence that's meaningful to you and related to your joy.

I am magick, and on Litha, I celebrate the expansive, colorful, and full expression of me. The disabled experience invites creative inclusion, and thus my joy is expansively creative. I invoke this power of Litha to celebrate the parts of me and my life that fill me with joy. Regardless of my spoons or symptoms, I am beautiful, beloved, and powerful—worthy of hope. I am magick, transforming disparate pieces into a sunflower-shaped mosaic of joy.

25. Wheel of the Year: A Lammas Ritual Centered on Disability

Lammas, celebrated on August 1, is about harvest and the approaching fall. It is a transformational time. Summer is waning, and the entirely different rhythms of fall are nascent. To me, this feels like a time to consider what I want in the year to come. This looks different for me as a disabled person—unlike those with a non-disabled experience, I can't always plan with meticulous detail and accuracy. But that doesn't mean I can't set intentions. Intentions, like all of witchcraft, are available for all.

This is a ritual of intention for the harvest, understood here metaphorically and referring to finding abundance in all of our varied experiences, centering the disabled experience in this context.

Before starting this ritual, consider the following questions:

- What does harvest time mean to you?

- In this liminal space between the typically more free-flowing summer and the typically more structured fall, which of the two do you feel most drawn to? Why?

- What parts of an abled harvest celebration do you have access to? What parts do you not have access to? How might you reclaim those elements and transform them using disabled witchcraft?

- As you consider what intentions you have seen come to harvest this year, what intentions do you wish to call in for next year?

[• • •]

What You'll Need for This Ritual:

- An item that represents harvest to you (for example, a fall leaf, fall decorations you already have, in-season fruit, etc.)

Hold the harvest item close to you in some way. Focus your energy on it. Infuse it with the following incantation of intention:

> *This Lammas, I harvest the ways I have already transformed an ableist world by my very existence. I infuse this item with this power and the following intentions: [add in your intentions from the discussion questions above]. In the complexity of living in an unjust system, I invoke my own love and power to bring these intentions into being. I am magick, and I am enough as I am.*

26. Wheel of the Year: A Mabon Ritual Centered on Disability

As I mentioned in the Ostara ritual (#22), I've always adored the word *equinox*, since long before I was formally practicing witchcraft.

And this is especially true of the autumn equinox, which is what Mabon commemorates on the Wheel of the Year. It is a harvest time. In this spirit, my Mabon ritual is focused on gratitude, including excitement for my favorite time of the year—fall, which holds so much personal meaning for me.

This ritual is designed to celebrate that anticipation and also to celebrate those beautiful things about spoonies that are so often overlooked and forgotten by non-disabled people, who often see disabled people as, at best, people to be pitied. It's about gratitude for the disabled community and all the bright and vibrant ways we show up, including in this mysterious and exciting time of Mabon.

[• • •]

What You'll Need for This Ritual:

- In-season produce or other food that is accessible and that you associate with this time of year

- Candle or other accessible alternative you associate with gratitude

Gather friends to eat this harvest meal together. At the beginning of the meal, light a candle or accessible alternative. Invite all participants to recite the following words of gratitude if they would like to:

This Mabon, we thank all who have gone before and all who will come after and all who are here now who uphold us with their love and strengthen us forward, empowering us to look with joy and gratitude at the magick that is. Today we have special gratitude for all in our number who are disabled and have transformed their worlds with the magick of their existence.

Chapter Five: Thrifty, Scrappy Rituals

One of the things that is so overlooked about disability in a capitalistic hellscape is the financial aspect. Healthcare is expensive, and on top of that, disabled people often can't work typical jobs that can cover those costs, especially while also leaving room for things like hobbies and even purchasing spiritually meaningful items for rituals.

Moreover, creating through scraps is such an act of disabled resistance. We know what it's like to be "thrown away" by society. So making our grimoires or ritual supplies out of old shit that needs some love is a transformative and disabled magickal act.

That's why this chapter is devoted to scrappy, thrifty, and creative rituals that can be adapted for any budget. Because witchcraft is for everyone.

27. Creating a Scrappy Grimoire When You Don't Have Money for That Gorgeous Handmade, Fair Trade Reclaimed Leather One Online...

Most witches keep some kind of notebook—virtual or otherwise—where they keep research, spells, and rituals they've read, developed, or experienced. This is often called a grimoire.

As witches, we seek to honor the earth through all of our practices, but as disabled people our budgets are limited.

If money were no object, I'd buy a gorgeous grimoire hand bound by well-paid artisans, wrapped in sustainably sourced reclaimed leather that wasn't harmfully processed, bound with ethically produced or recycled natural fiber thread, and made with recycled paper. It would be fully compostable or reusable and would also be made to last.

But I do not have the budget for this perfectionistic (if lovely and ideal) dream.

As a disabled person on a limited budget, I've sourced grimoire notebooks a number of ways, and I work to make sure I never feel shame about them. My goal is to become more and more mindful and respectful in how I procure witchy supplies, and part of that mindfulness comes in being aware of my own budget, spoons, and resources.

However you make your grimoire, you are enough, resisting by your very existence.

Here are just a few ideas . . .

- Sometimes you luck out and find a gorgeous journal at a thrift store or in a Buy Nothing group. This is a great way to use something that already exists and honor the earth through a form of recycling.

- For the times when spoons are few and budgets are small, avail yourself of the dollar store and other discount retailers, especially around back-to-school season, when the savings are often the greatest. A $1 grimoire is still a grimoire. My first grimoire was a small, pretty moon-themed journal I found at the dollar store near my house. It served me really well when I was a baby witch.

- Keep a digital grimoire. You can make a lovely grimoire virtually for free using whatever word processing and text apps are available on your devices. Thanks to screen readers, this could be a great option for blind witches or those with low vision. And if you ever do want to print it out, you can always do so at your local library. You could even create a Pinterest board of rituals you've learned from other witchy creators online.

- Consider making an auditory grimoire by recording your spells and magickal findings. Or consider a multisensory, 3D grimoire (stored in whatever way is accessible to you) that organizes your practices using a collection of paper, fabric, nature items, and other meaningful pieces that express your magickal intentions through touch or other senses.

- Sometimes I find inexpensive books destined for the garbage at thrift stores or at overstock/returns stores and rehab them into grimoires. This is especially satisfying when the book was originally racist, sexist, ableist, fatphobic, homophobic, transphobic, classist, etc. Basically, I find cheap reclaimed leather scraps on Etsy, hot glue them around the covers, use thrifted or inexpensive stickers and old papers to cover up the problematic bits of text and give me space to write, and voila … a grimoire!

- If you're really fancy and have a lot of spoons and a craft budget, you can try binding your own grimoires. I tried this once (it's how I got the idea for the above bullet point), using *Make Your Own Ideabook with Arne and Carlos: Create Handmade Art Journals and Bound Keepsakes to Store Inspiration and Memories* by Arne Nerjordet and Carlos Zachrison, which I borrowed from my local library. I've found libraries often have amazing art how-to books that you can borrow for free and get lots of inspiration from. As great as Pinterest is, I'm a sucker for the tactile experience of holding a book and creating something with it, hence my love of grimoires.

When you have your grimoire in hand, you can use the following incantation to welcome it:

Oh scrappy grimoire, I consecrate you.

You are magick, transformed to enable more transformation.

I used my power to create you, and your scrappy
self is connected by all your disparate parts to
so many who have gone before.

This is the magick of disabled creativity.

28. Secondhand Craft: Thrifting as Ritual When Funds Are Tight

Have you ever felt the pressure to buy lots of witchy shit?
Me too.

Look, I'm as susceptible as anyone to overconsumption
in a world where we are bombarded with ads 24/7. Is it
any wonder that consumerism permeates our spirituality
too?

But we also have needs, whether it's feeding our bodies
or finding a creative hobby to take care of our mental
health. And in our capitalist society, that typically means
buying something.

As witches, honoring the earth and our connection to
it is central to our spiritual walk, and that's as true now as
it has ever been, given the effects of climate change. This
is often in tension with the need to buy things.

And then add disability into this ethical quagmire. How
can you afford to buy ethically made witchy paraphernalia
when you can barely afford rent because of medical bills
and low wages that often make even non-disabled humans
unable to meet their needs?

Thrifting is one mindful, witchy way that I seek to get my needs met and express myself creatively. I'm taking resources that already exist and finding in them abundance, rebirth, and hope. It's transformative work.

It's taking a five-year-old T-shirt and giving it a new life and styling.

It's finding a pair of gorgeous earrings that look like they could have been part of the iconic outfits of *The Craft* but that need some replacement rhinestones, which you already happen to have in your when-I-have-spoons arts-and-craft bin.

It's finding your partner a pair of desperately needed running shorts.

It's finding, in the bulk bins, a high-quality pair of mittens that you would never be able to afford normally; they just need a quick bath and some stitching on one side.

And to expand this even more, it's bartering with others. Giving and receiving in a Buy Nothing group, Freecycle, or a free store. Saving clothes bins for your grandchildren and neighborhood kids to cycle through for free. Using your friend's old yoga mat when they need to buy a specialized one for health reasons. Donating good books you're no longer reading to the library. Swapping clothes with your housemate.

It's transforming nothing into something. It's the witchcraft of community and connection.

Next time you have the spoons to pursue thrifting or secondhanding, consider the following questions:

- What do you need—clothing, entertainment, tools for creative endeavors or other practical concerns, books?

- What resources does your community have to help you as you work together to transform nothing into something?

Before you head out on your adventure, say the following incantation:

> *Today, I am worthy of all that I need. I am worthy of finding the beauty in the unexpected and considering beautiful things that spark my interest. I am worthy of the help of my community. May I have discernment to know what is for me and what does not serve me. May I find what I can through secondhand means, as much as possible. May I hold space for fulfilling all my needs in whatever ways I can. May I have opportunities to both give and take in the alchemy of sharing, reusing, transforming what is here now.*

29. Remaking: A Transformation Ritual

I have always adored upcycling, long before I even knew what that word was.

As a child, I would take cardboard boxes, old catalogues, staples, pens, and markers and turn recyclables into dollhouses, doll candy stores, and doghouses for plushie pets.

As a teen, I went to art fairs and was in awe of guitar picks turned into necklaces, beer bottles turned into earrings, juice pouches turned into purses, plastic bags turned into plarn, duct tape turned into wallets, old paper wrapped into beads, old fabric turned into scrappy quilts.

At my wedding, I reused old silk flowers and books for décor and carried flowers made out of actual old books.

As an adult, I turned a dilapidated pair of shorts into a pocket cross-body bag, scrap yarn and fabric pieces into games for my niblings, problematic books into art journal grimoires, thrifted plastic Christmas wreaths into spell jars and ornaments.

It turns out I'm not the only one who sees the magick in upcycling. Judy Rom, curator of *Upcycle That*, a blog about creative ways to repurpose items, says this: "Upcycling is alchemy. By creatively repurposing and reusing, we can turn trash into treasure."

Upcycling has the potential for such accessibility. It's about transformation, resourcefulness, frugality, and using what you've got—skills born out of necessity for disabled witches. The magick of transformation here is only helped by the witchy proclivity to infuse intentions into every little thing we're up to.

Do you have items in your house that you'd like to repurpose? What tools are available for you to do that? What is accessible for you to do?

It doesn't have to be anything super complex. Maybe turn a beautiful piece of printed cardboard from a snack box into a bookmark? Maybe use an old frame to house flowers pressed from your yard? Maybe old junk mail could be cut up into confetti for a mosaic or for throwing during an indoor celebration? Maybe old scrap paper could house doodles or shopping lists or notes at the next doctor's visit?

The goal of this remaking ritual is not perfection, but transformation. Taking something you already have and turning it into something you want or need—something that will bring practicality, joy, or both into your life.

Once you have found your project, select an intention to infuse in the steps. When your project is finished, repeat the following:

My intention is to [state your intention].

I transform this item into something new with the magick of upcycling, brought about by the power of my own creativity, resourcefulness, and ingenuity. I am magick.

30. Weaving a Crown of Intentions for Abundant Hope

What does abundance mean for a disabled, anti-capitalist person? It was a question I was pondering as I wrote and researched this book.

One morning, while pulling cards, I encountered a beautiful "gatherer invocation" in Juliet Diaz and Lorraine Anderson's *The Earthcraft Oracle Guidebook* that encouraged seeing "abundance all around."

Yes, true abundance is about being resourceful and creative. And scrappy, resourceful, and creative rituals infused with intention have always been my favorite. One of my earliest clues about my witchiness was how I infused meaning, intention, magick, and spirituality into my clothing choices, including when I began making flower crowns for fun around 2015. I remember my first crown was a mix of red flowers, yellow flowers, and green leaves that I found at the craft store (allergies suck). I chose yellow as a symbol of hope in my life due to some spiritual experiences I had had. I chose the green leaves as a symbol of growth and new happenings (I was almost done with my undergrad and in a serious and healthy romantic relationship), and I chose the red flowers as a symbol of love in my life (we were slowly approaching engagement at that time).

The beauty of flower crowns is that they can be used for any intention and are accessible in their ability to transform whatever is readily available into beautiful, intention-filled magickal wearables or décor.

As witchy spoonies—resourceful and transformative—we are witches of abundant hope. Consider making a flower crown of your own for your intentions. If you've never made a flower crown, there are many ways to do it, and different people prefer different methods, so I recommend checking out YouTube and Pinterest to find your preferred method.

As you make your crown, weave in intentions about a more inclusive world and space. Here are some possibilities for what you could visualize:

- Laws that would create more inclusive spaces (and the necessary resources, time, or help to make those laws happen)

- Celebrations of the beautiful diversity within the disabled community and within humanity in general

- Accommodations you hope for soon (and the practical steps that may need to happen for those to become a reality)

- Your success, what that means to you, and all the different ways it might be possible

- What abundance would mean for you and/or for society as a whole beyond the constraints of capitalist and ableist expectations

After weaving your crown, you can wear it for the rest of the day (or future witchy holidays). Or you can display it somewhere prominent that will remind you of your intentions in the days and weeks to come. (If the flowers are real, drying it to preserve it as a display or to wear to future witchy holidays is one option.)

31. Mending: A Ritual for You, Your Bank Account, and the Earth

With disability, money is often tight (due to medical bills and few options for accommodating jobs to earn much-needed cash) and traditional channels of climate activism (like protests) aren't always accessible. Enter: mending.

I love mending as ritual because it does more than one thing at once: (1) it resists unjust systems that exploit the earth and the creatures that inhabit it and (2) it saves money. It does these things by preserving what we have, using limited resources to do that.

For a lot of mending projects, like small holes in bags, shirts, and pants, all you need is similar scrap fabric, some thread, scissors, and some needles of different sizes—all of which you may already have lying around. As for skills, a whip stitch and a straight stitch will get you far.

I'm not a good sewist by any means, but I've mended a lot of things over the years (still can't hem pants though, sorry to say). I've tried to be creative about using the thread and needles I had from a cheap sewing kit that was given to me secondhand.

Sewing in particular presents an amazing opportunity for ritual. With each stitch, we can infuse intention. By selecting the color of the thread, we can infuse correspondences. And with each project, we are transforming what our capitalist society would view as trash into something that can continue to survive the test of time.

So next time you mend, consider your intentions and correspondences, infusing your work with the magick that is you.[18]

For a mending ritual, all you really need is yourself and any sewing supplies necessary for the repair, but these reflection questions can guide you into making it your own:

- With this project, what item(s) are you working to mend? What purpose does this item serve?

- Are there any meaningful color, texture, or design correspondences in the item(s) you are mending?

- What are the intentions you've infused or correspondences you associate with the thread (or other tools) you've chosen for this project?

---

18 A note about spoons: There are times when I can't mend because of pain, and if I must mend, I spread it out into small sessions—a few stitches here and there. I also don't subscribe to any perfectionistic beliefs about mending. I'm not an expert, so each new attempt is a learning-by-doing experience. Know that whatever you can or can't get done with mending is enough. This is about intention, ritual, and action, not perfection.

Keep these intentions and correspondences at the forefront of your mind. When you're ready to start the mending, begin with this short mending spell:

With every stitch
I resist
Disabled, crafty witch
I call in the love of all who have gone before
And all who come after
To make something new again
To make it into something new
I call in this power
And rest in my own magick
To make meaning
To mend.

Chapter Six: Artistic Rituals

*T*firmly believe creativity is magick, and as I've mentioned earlier in this book, I believe that we as disabled witches are a uniquely creative and resourceful group. In this chapter, I'm including some art rituals that have been meaningful to me. I invite disabled witches everywhere to adapt these and make your own magick from art and creativity.

32. Crafting a Story: A Ritual for Delighting Your Inner Child

Spoonies are a creative and whimsical bunch, in my experience. We find joy in the mundane and small. We are resourceful because we have to be, finding the closest thing to accommodation that we can to survive and thrive. In a word, spoonies have the power and magick of imagination—on a small scale but also in imagining a better world.

I believe imagination is itself magick.

It likely comes as no surprise that I enjoy writing fiction. And the reason I do is because it's always been a place for me to explore what a better world might look like. To find humor, joy, questions, answers, ways of being, and more in a safe, expansive place.

I invite you to craft a story. It can be short. Stories only need a beginning, middle, and end.

For this ritual, you really don't need anything other than your own imagination, but a digital or physical journal can be great.

If you need a creative prompt, consider (1) your favorite part of life and (2) the ways that part is not accessible to all. Then answer this question in your story: "What if it was accessible? What would it look like? What beauty, joy, silliness, hope might be possible then?"

If you're new to writing stories, set a timer for ten minutes and see what you come up with. Remember that you're connecting to what it is like to be a kid. When kids are free to play, their stories and imaginations are boundless, nonsensical, silly, and even serious all at once. There is no right or wrong here. Only whimsy and hope.

When your story is done, consider gathering your fellow spoonies, witches, or other community members and sharing your story. You might even consider having a story ritual gathering where you all write stories and share them as you desire.

Because there is magick in storytelling. It's powerful, and stories are most powerful when they're shared, even if you just share them with yourself.

You are enough, dear witchy spoonie storyteller.

33. Color Magick for Comfortable Clothes

I love fashion and color, so one of my favorite forms of magick is color magick, especially with my outfits. Color magick is basically imbuing your intentions into the colors of clothes, décor, or other areas of your life or rituals. On decent spoon days, I love putting together outfits with color correspondences that are meaningful to me—equal parts introspectively inspirational and outwardly expressive.

But sometimes when pain prevents me from wearing what I want to wear, the clothes I wear feel like anything but an artful expression. This is where color magick can really shine. Even when I'm wearing comfortable but inexpressive clothes that are less than fun—that feel like comfort but not so much like me—I use color as a way to invoke those same ideas. Red for love, black for strength and protection, green for vitality and groundedness, blue for authenticity, etc.

Take a look at your comfy clothes that you use for pain days. What colors are they? Do they feel like you? Is there a way you can make them feel like you by adding a patch, drawing something with a fabric marker, or adding a comfortable accessory like a scarf, loose necklace, or hypoallergenic earrings?

And whatever you do or wear, even if there are no spoons or funds or resources to adapt or grow your comfy wardrobe, you can infuse it with intention by following these steps:

1. Bring the item close to you.

2. Reflect on it for a moment, imagining energy transferring from you into the clothing.

3. Visualize the intention you want to infuse.

4. Wear the item, knowing your power is within it, simply because it is connected to you.

34. Creating Art Infused with Wholeness Intentions

The word *healing*, in a spiritual context, can be triggering for me. Often, instead of advocating for policies, practices, and accommodations that would actually help disabled people, many spiritual groups will simply pray for healing, imply that the disabled person doesn't have enough faith, and/or charge exorbitant sums of money for what often amounts to a placebo effect (if that).

While I'm a deeply spiritual person who does find a sort of healing in my spirituality, it has always been in tandem with medical solutions and accommodations. Spiritual and physical are not separate, in my view. That's why, instead of healing, I often prefer the term *wholeness*. Because, disabled or not, I am whole. While I live in a society that does not accommodate me, there is nothing wrong or bad about me. I am simply a disabled human living in a capitalist world. I am enough.

In the swirl of misdiagnoses, new appointments, and unexpected symptoms, I find hope and a sense of my own wholeness through art. I infuse wholeness intentions in whatever creative project I'm working on. And I'm as eclectic in my art as I am in my witchcraft. I dabble in poetry, fiction, painting, hand embroidery, sewing, contemplative coloring, doll DIYs, gallery walls, and art journaling. I've even tried knitting and crocheting multiple times, though no one has been able to successfully teach me (though many have tried).

I think creativity reflects wholeness to me because it allows me to express my experience without perfectionism, allowing me to show up as I am. Even if my art journals are eclectic and chaotic (which they usually are), even if my stitching is anything but straight (what else is new?), even if my projects go uncompleted (because spoons are a thing, even for hobbies), it all says, "I'm enough, not defined or made valuable by the ableist systems I'm a part of."

Now comes the fun part. If art as a wholeness ritual appeals to you, decide on an artistic project (or several projects) that you'd like to create, and gather the necessary supplies. (Many thrift stores have inexpensive craft sections, and Buy Nothing groups often have craft supplies too. I've even seen witch groups do craft supply swap events.)

Once you've chosen your art project and gathered your supplies, lay the supplies out before you and repeat the following incantation:

> *Imperfect or exact, what I create is good and*
> *enough. I infuse these supplies and these*
> *projects with one intention: the recognition of*
> *my wholeness as a disabled human. This art is*

a magickal act declaring that my power and my
magick are enough as they are. This expression
is the magick.

35. Cut It Up: A Transformative Ritual Against Violent, Ableist Words

I don't believe in book banning; I'm too marginalized as a queer and disabled witch to think censorship is a good idea. Instead, I believe in facilitating conversations (or exiting conversations if you're in an unsafe situation). But I wrestle with how to do this when I come up against words that are ableist or that otherwise prop up the shitstorm of unjust systems that surround us. If I want to engage with ableist words or am forced to (and have the spoons to do so), how do I work with this?

I got the idea for this ritual while attending a lovely poetry workshop created and led by Cara Meredith and Marla Taviano[19] called "Upcycling Words That No Longer Fit," at which a group of mostly exvangelical writers gathered together to engage with and transform problematic words that we'd read, that had been said to us, and even that we had written. If that level of transformation isn't witchcraft, I don't know what is!

---

19 While neither Marla nor Cara are witches, they both write a lot of amazing spirituality content and are both always up to new and interesting creative endeavors, so I just had to give these writer friends of mine a shout-out. You can find out more about their work at CaraMeredith.com and MarlaTaviano.com.

One of the practices we did was cut-up poetry, where you take words and phrases cut out of preexisting materials and use them to create a sort of mosaic poem. This is the practice we're going to use in this ritual.

So what are some texts in your life that are ableist or otherwise problematic? Now is an opportunity to reclaim and transform them through the witchcraft of poetry.

[• • •]

What You'll Need for This Ritual:

- A problematic text of some sort
- A way to digitally or physically cut up that text and arrange the phrases and words to create a poem

When you're done creating your poem, not only will you have the catharsis of destroying and transforming ableist words, you'll also have a poem, which you could also use as an anti-ableist incantation for your own creative rituals.

36. Ideas of Joy: A Low-Spoons Poetic Ritual

When you think about a poem, what comes to mind? For me, it's images—crystallized ideas that capture a metaphor in few words. I love the way poet Rachel Richardson describes the relationship between imagery and poetry in an article for the Poetry Foundation: "You can think of imagery as an entryway into a poem: a physical realm allowing us to explore the mind of the poet."

As someone who's naturally drawn to poetry and who carries so many evocative experiences as a disabled and queer person, I found in witchcraft a truly poetic ritual expression. Witchcraft is so much about visualization—about noticing—that poetry is a natural fit.

But you don't have to be the poet type to connect with this ritual. This is meant to be infinitely customizable to your own experience.

As disabled people, we walk a difficult road because of the ableist world we exist in. And yet we have joy in our lives, flying in the face of ableist pity and patronizing platitudes.

For this ritual, consider images or ideas that bring you joy. They could be actual pictures (digital or printed), they could be memories, they could be descriptive scenes from your favorite book or show, they could be trinkets that you use for your hobbies or have received or given as gifts.

Take these images of joy and arrange them in some way: in a digital collage, in a gallery wall, as drawings in a sketchbook, as a visualization you keep in your mind, or even as a poem. Keep the final product somewhere for whenever you need a visual intention of resistance through your existence. Let this collection of comforting and strengthening ideas, images, or items serve as a magickal resource for you whenever you need some joy.

37. Art Journaling: A Ritual for Finding Joy with Help from Others

One practice that has buoyed me through many a spoonless night is remembering an important fact: I do not have to fucking do this alone.

Enter art journaling: for me, this practice is collage making to the extreme, gathering words, pictures, stickers, quotes, lyrics, and more—from others who have inspired me and given me hope through the beauty they have brought into the world just by being themselves.

As a person whose job it is to be creative, sometimes I need a moment to not worry about making everything from scratch, but to rely on the love and creativity of others in a chaotically beautiful collage that reminds me that I am not alone. When I flip through the pages of my art journals, I see love, I see beauty, and I see hope. And I see that I am not fucking alone. That there is a mosaic of love, of connection, of experience swirling around me, upholding me, strengthening me.

[• • •]

What You'll Need for This Ritual:

- Some kind of page(s) to affix the pieces of your art journal collage to (journal, scrap paper, etc.)

- Anything you want to incorporate into your art journal (stickers, magazines, fabric scraps, quotes you like, words you like, markers/other accessible writing utensils, etc.)

- Any adhesive or cutting tools that are accessible to you (tape, glue sticks, etc.)

Once you've gathered your supplies, begin the ritual with these words, spoken over your tools:

O disparate pieces of beauty and connection, I transform you into a rainbow-hued collective voice, declaring a reality bigger than the sum of its parts. I call upon the magick of the love of all who have contributed to the raw materials of my art journal pages. I thank them for their work, and I honor and transform and participate now in a magickal way. I infuse my energy, my magick into these pages.

Now is the time to create.

Once you're done creating your art journal, repeat these words:

Behold! I have transformed and combined, showing the connection of all. I have declared my experience and the experience of many through the magick of art. I have taken disparate pieces, forgotten pieces, even repurposed pieces deemed by some to be useless

trash and have created beauty, resistance,
expression. And this is the magick of me, a
disabled person, crushing binaries and creating
connection just by my very existence, as shown
in the microcosm that is my mosaic art.

38. Witchy Painting

Have you ever noticed how much paint brushes look like wands? No wonder this art form is so magickal.

I started painting in 2019 and did a lot during 2020. It was one of the only art forms that worked with my pain symptoms at the time. For some reason, painting worked as a relaxing and low-spoon activity during those days. For paint, I used Natural Earth paints as well as spices and foods (like turmeric, coffee grounds, and spinach), and I also thrifted some less-natural paint for other projects. Whatever paint you use, you have the opportunity to transform a blank page into an intention-infused piece of art.

My favorite form of witchy painting was what I called "intention painting." I found a quote or phrase or other intention-adjacent words and used a pencil to write those on my paper. Then I traced the intention with my paint. Then I covered the intention with a painting of something that represented it. For example, as I flip through my notebook of painting, I see simple paintings of a dove, trees, a flower crown, and a globe of earth, each of which represents an intention written underneath. Sometimes the representation can just be a color, like in an angry painting I did at the close of 2020 against the injustice of the world. On a piece of cardboard from the recycling bin, I wrote out words that related to 2020 and what I wanted for the world going forward, then painted over those words with a haze of dumpster-fire reds and oranges. Simply put, this work does not need to be idyllic or complex. (I'm not a trained painter and most of my paintings look like doodles and scribbles.) Instead, it's about infusing transformative intentions with each stroke and color selection.

To conduct an intention-painting ritual:

- Gather the painting materials you have available to you. If none are available, are there accessible alternatives? Or is there a similar art activity you could do? For example, would a digital painting app be more accessible? Or would visualizing painting work better for you?

- Determine the intentions you want to infuse in the painting, especially as it relates to disability justice and/or your own experiences. For example, what parts of life would you like to see transformed into non-ableist spaces?

- Begin the painting process, visualizing your intentions. What correspondences of color or texture do you want to include? What images would represent the transformation you are seeking to bring about?

- When you are finished painting, place the painting in a location where you will see it so you can be reminded of your intentions and imbue your day-to-day life with those goals and dreams. If you visualized this painting for accessibility reasons, find a way to regularly remember a word or texture or color or other correspondence from it in the same way.

39. Bead Sigils

I recently got into making beaded friendship bracelets, after attending a lovely Taylor Swift friendship-bracelet-making party at Bettie's Pages, a fabulous bookstore and third space[20] in my area. I didn't get to go see the Eras Tour, so this was a fun way to participate. Someone brought their stash of beads and shared them with the community, and it was a lot of fun to work together on friendship bracelets of all themes—not just Taylor Swift.

One thing that immediately struck me was how multisensory beads are, especially the ones with letters stamped into them. That made me think about how accessible working with beads can be for any disability related to sensory stuff, whether that's forms of neurodivergence or forms of disability where touch is used more than another sense (such as sight). From a witchy perspective, I also quickly realized how beads (in bracelet form or not) reminded me of sigils—typically written

20 Third spaces are shared spaces that are neither home nor work. Examples of third spaces include stores, libraries, parks, and places of worship.

symbols that are highly individualized to specific witchy practitioners and involve intention and magickal meaning. Bracelet making is deeply personal and also includes 3D symbols: beads.

And so, I went on to start making deeply intentional friendship bracelets as sigils. But bead sigils don't have to be bracelets specifically: if beading a piece of jewelry is inaccessible to you, consider taking one bead (or a few) and keeping it (or them) close to you.

[• • •]

What You'll Need for This Ritual:

- Beads, buttons, or other accessible alternatives

- Optional: elastic cord for bracelet making

As you select your beads, fill them with intention. How does the color or texture of a bead remind you of intentions you may want to work with, especially with regard to disability inclusion? If you have letter beads, what words or partial words could you include to communicate your intentions?

As you gather the beads into a container that you can access easily, or arrange the beads around an altar space, or string the beads into jewelry, visualize your intentions so that whether you're making something wearable, sensory, or both, you can have a constant reminder of them—no matter what situations you find yourself in as a disabled person.

Chapter Seven: Disability Tarot Readings

*I*n this next chapter, we'll dive into the world of tarot. Tarot cards are used in many ways by many witchy people. For me, I use tarot (in addition to other types of witchy oracle decks) as a tool to give me prompts and invitations to listen to my intuition, usually drawing a card in the morning. I don't view tarot or other forms of divination as immutable, for-sure things. Instead, I view them as an invitation and prompt to consider what our own intuition knows. Divination is a tool that can help us shore up knowledge from within ourselves that might otherwise be cloudy for any number of reasons.

Every witch's practice is different, but typically the practitioner will begin by asking a question (e.g., "How can I take care of myself as a spoonie in my current situation?"), then give a reading using any number of structures they deem best. In my case, I like to do single-card readings and use them as prompts to get people in touch with their intuition, and that's what I'll be doing here, from a disability lens. To keep things simple, I won't be getting into how cards can be read depending on which way they face out when drawn. This is a fascinating part of tarot, but for this chapter, I will be focusing on very simplified single-card readings, zeroing in on one aspect or possible meaning of each card.

Tarot cards are divided into two parts: the major arcana and the minor arcana. The major arcana includes twenty-two cards displaying archetypes that, in order, can tell the story of the journey of the main character, called the fool, which is the first card in the major arcana. The minor arcana cards include the four major suits—wands, cups, swords, and pentacles. Each suit has its own focus for meaning, which we'll get into in the minor arcana readings in this chapter. For simplicity, we will not be going through each card in the suit; instead, we will be doing one reading for each suit to explore the broad focus of that suit as it could relate to disability.

(If you're new to tarot and want to dig deeper into the meanings associated with each of the cards, I recommend Tina Gong's *Tarot: Connect with Yourself, Develop Your Intuition, Live Mindfully* and the tarot resource section in Friday Gladheart's *The Practical Witch's Almanac 2024: Grow Your Craft*.)

40. Disability and Tarot: A Reading from the Fool Card (Major Arcana 0)

We begin with the fool, which, according to Tina Gong's *Tarot*, can be positively interpreted to mean "optimism," "new beginnings," "potential," and "freedom."

Like the fool, the disabled experience is characterized by resourcefulness on a journey, with infinite possibilities for creative solutions that lead to increased community and freedom. We survive not on uncritical optimism, but on a kind of hope that comes from our community's magick.

When we are handed shitty systems along our journey, we transform the scraps we are given into community and accessibility, with an optimism and awareness of potential characterized by the fool card. We transform ableist expectations with joy, acceptance, celebration, and inclusivity.

The fool, then, is a harbinger of joy and subverted expectations.

If you draw the fool, consider:

- How does your existence bring joy to you and your community?

- In what ways have your own experiences given you freedom from ableist expectations? In what ways would you like to invoke and assert more freedom in your life and in the life of your community and the world?

- In what ways have you already transformed through the magick of disabled witchcraft, subverting ableist assumptions?

- What fool-centered intentions could you infuse in your rituals today?

41. Disability and Tarot: A Reading from the Magician Card (Major Arcana 1)

We now move on to the magician, and what a fucking awesome card it is to draw!

As a big kidlit and tarot fan, a recent fun find for me was Abigail Samoun's *Tarot for Baby*, which has a lot of whimsical, sweet, and simple interpretations of the major arcana that I think apply to the experience of all humans, well beyond babyhood. I especially love how she interprets the magician card as a rallying cry for the titular baby (and for any readers too): "Fear not, brave one—you have everything you need!"

Throughout the rituals in this book, I've emphasized the idea that disabled people are magickal in and of themselves because of the transformative power their experiences bring to ableist spaces.

And so, dear disabled, witchy spoonie, you are a magician. Don't ever forget that.

Your scrappiness, your courage, your resourcefulness, your care for yourself have not gone unnoticed and have not been in vain. When you pull this card, remember that no matter what degrading and dehumanizing things are said and done by the capitalist system—no fucking matter what—you are magickal and you are transforming just by being.

When you draw the magician card, consider the following:

- When did you first see yourself as a witch or magickal practitioner? What makes you feel magickal in your practice?

- How much do you believe that you are magickal as you are?

- What intentions could you infuse into your rituals and routines that would remind you of this truth?

42. Disability and Tarot: A Reading from the High Priestess Card (Major Arcana 2)

Now we look at the high priestess card. I like one message that Tarot.com draws from this card: "Put self-cultivation at the top of your daily priority list."

In an ableist society, daily care for our bodies is at the bottom of the list, crushed under profit and greed. Witchy spoonies, armed with the high priestess card, are invited to perform the magick of self-care: the daily tasks of food, drink, medicine, shelter, bathing, sleep, stretching, moving, deep breathing, journaling, going to therapy, etc.—all infused with magickal intentions.

If you pulled this card today, consider the following questions:

- In what ways are you caring for yourself on a micro level? What mundane day-to-day self-care practices and must-dos do you have space to attend to?

- In what ways are you caring for yourself on a macro level? Are there systems, jobs, or other major factors in your life that might not be serving your care? If so, what would I want instead? What might be possible to change over time?

In what ways are you trusting yourself and your own wisdom and magick as a high priestess in your life? What needs of yours might your intuition be bringing to mind that need care right now?

43. Disability and Tarot: A Reading from the Empress Card (Major Arcana 3)

Today, we turn to the empress card. One of my favorite tarot decks ever is *The Antique Anatomy Tarot* by Claire Goodchild, which incorporates beautiful illustrations of human anatomy, intermingled with blooming flowers and plants. There is something so beautifully disabled about this deck's deconstruction of the beauty of every body and all of our connections to the earth. In the guidebook that accompanies this deck, Goodchild writes, "The Empress greets you with warmth, beauty, and motherly love."

I love this invitation to love ourselves, finding care we may not have otherwise received in the empress, which I believe represents self-love and the love of all our ancestors, God, and nature—all that mysterious connection.

When an ableist world tries to convince you that you are anything but a fucking magickal masterpiece—

beloved, disabled, whole, and transforming—the empress card declares that we are all royalty.

If you pull the empress card, consider the following questions:

- What parts of your body do you see beauty in? What parts do you struggle to see beauty in?

- What has ableist society told you about your body and your worth? What intentions of self-love could you work into your witchy practice to counteract these harmful messages?

- In what small ways can you remind yourself of your own royalty and the royalty of all others? (For example, consider making an intention-filled flower crown, collage, or outfit.)

44. Disability and Tarot: A Reading from the Emperor Card (Major Arcana 4)

One thing I love about tarot is its ability to represent the spectrum of identities. There is both an empress and an emperor card, showing the range of gender expression that we all can have. Today, we turn to the latter.

According to Sophie Saint Thomas, *Allure's* resident astrologer and witchcraft author, "Drawing The Emperor could indicate the advantage of adding more structure to your life."

As a disabled person, (flexible) routines have been very helpful to me. They help me prioritize what is and isn't important to get done each day to take care of myself. Drawing this card may be an opportunity to assess your routines or try new routines that might work better for you personally—because all spoonies are unique and have unique needs for care and routine. Because you, witchy spoonie, are royal stardust, magickal and worthy of care, connected to all others (who are also royalty).

If you drew the emperor, consider the following questions:

- What routines are and aren't working for you and your needs?

- Are there routines you want to implement but haven't been able to?

- What accommodations or modified versions of these routines could you try? What people in your life could you reach out to for support in working toward these goals?

45. Disability and Tarot: A Reading from the Hierophant Card (Major Arcana 5)

Today, we consider the hierophant and how this card connects to disability. I love the way TheTarotGuide.com, a free resource for learning about tarot, describes one of this card's meanings: "knowledge sharing."

I can think of no better description for the disabled community. We are knowledge sharers, a community of hierophants who disseminate knowledge—about available accommodations, treatments, and helpful or unhelpful medical providers—in order to help our fellow disabled hierophants and allies. What a remarkable and magickal community!

So, if you draw the hierophant card, consider the following questions:

- How have you benefitted from knowledge shared by your fellow disabled hierophants?

- How have you shared knowledge as a disabled hierophant?

- In what ways can you give support going forward? In what ways can you continue to receive support in the community?

46. Disability and Tarot: A Reading from the Lovers Card (Major Arcana 6)

Today, we turn to an ever-popular card: the lovers. One of the most fascinating things about this card is how broad its interpretation can be. Meghan Rose, a spiritual advisor and tarot reader in California, shared this expansive meaning for this card in an article for *Glamour*: "partnerships (romantic or business)." I would expand it even further to encompass all kinds of partnerships. Love and community take many forms, and those partnerships are vital for our survival as humans and as witchy spoonies.

If you draw the lovers card, consider the following questions:

- What is your community like? Who is a part of it?

- What are your desires for partnership (business, romantic, sexual, friendship, self-love, etc.)? What beautiful things do you bring to a partnership just by being your magickal, disabled self?

- How can you work on yourself to be a more and more loving partner who takes care of your needs and the needs of any partners?

- How can you infuse your intentions for love into your rituals and life?

- What accommodations might you need on this journey?

47. Disability and Tarot: A Reading from the Chariot Card (Major Arcana 7)

We now turn to the chariot card.

Sarah Regan, the spirituality and relationships editor for Mind Body Green, writes that the chariot card "represents empowerment, achievement, overcoming obstacles, and triumph."

In the disability space, some of those words are fucking triggering because of the tendency for ableist society to view us as nothing more than inspiration . . . and to silence experiences that aren't what they deem inspirational. (And don't even get me started on disability in the Christian church.[21])

The disabled experience is complex. It's not a monolith. It's not just conquering obstacles, it's calling out when the system is itself an obstacle. It's bad spoon days, shitty providers, amazing providers, amazing found family, organizing for change in accessible ways, health insurance admin, and so much more.

So when you pull the chariot card, consider the following questions:

- In what ways do you inspire yourself and others? How do you feel about this?

- What accommodations would make it so your life didn't have to be "inspirational"?

- What accommodations and safe found community exist in your life and world now?

- How can you honor the complexity of the disabled experience in your rituals, remembering that you are magick and enough as you are?

48. Disability and Tarot: A Reading from the Strength Card (Major Arcana 8)

We now look at the strength card. In *Kawaii Tarot: Understanding Tarot with the Kawaii Universe*, written by Chris Barsanti and illustrated by Lulu Mayo, we find the

21 For an excellent primer on that, check out My Body Is Not a Prayer Request by Dr. Amy Kenny.

strength card adorably reinterpreted as a cat balancing a mouse friend upon their head while surrounded by other creatures. The closing reflection reads "You have strength. But what does that mean to you?"

Finding a personal definition of strength according to our own values is challenging enough when we're non-disabled within a capitalist system. But to be disabled is to upend societal expectations of strength in a much more extreme way.

We are resilient in ways we never should've had to be, AND we need accommodations to do many "basic" things. We balance much AND are surrounded by both insensitive gawkers and loving communities.

If you draw this card, consider the following questions:

- How do you define strength in others? In yourself?

- How have you shown strength in unexpected and magickal ways as a disabled person?

- How does your community give you strength? How do you provide strength to others just by existing?

49. Disability and Tarot: A Reading from the Hermit Card (Major Arcana 9)

We now turn our attention to the hermit card. In the beautiful *The Tarot Journal* by Melissa Turnberry, several keywords are listed in relation to this card: "solitude, withdrawal, detachment, caution, patience, prudence, discretion, limitation." And I think all of those words connect with so many of our disabled experiences.

This card is an invitation to the quiet power of rest—of consideration for our spoons, regardless of societal pressure to do and be beyond any reasonable human ability. This card's magick is in its marginalization. The hermit stands in direct contrast to the hustle and bustle of capitalism—quiet rest and relaxation are vital to the magickal experience of being alive.

Today, if you draw this card, consider the following:

- How are you embodying the magick of the hermit in your rhythms of life?

- How many spoons do you have today?

- What hermit-centered intentions can you infuse in your rituals for the day to acknowledge and hold space for your spoons as they are?

50. Disability and Tarot: A Reading from the Wheel of Fortune Card (Major Arcana 10)

We now turn our attention to the wheel of fortune card. In *Tarot for Change*, Jessica Dore, licensed social worker and tarot reader, says of this card: "The Wheel of Fortune is a symbol of change and it's also a symbol of evolution; its circular shape symbolizes the marriage of opposites."

From the disabled experience, I see this on such a deep level. While change is inevitable, there is something about being disabled in an ableist world that is so ever-changing, so non-monolithic. Diagnoses change, insurances change, providers change, symptoms change, spoon levels change—but through it all, we the disabled are whole people. While *whole* and *disabled* might seem like opposites, they are actually part of the wheel of the disabled experience.

If you draw this card, consider the following:

- What things seem like opposites?

- How does your life magickally connect these opposites?

- How do these mysterious pairings appear through your disabled witchcraft or other forms of witchcraft?

51. Disability and Tarot: A Reading from the Justice Card (Major Arcana II)

Behold, we now turn to the justice card. And what a fucking powerful card to pull in relation to the disabled experience! To just add one other layer from my own experience, I'm also bringing queerness into this. Because justice is intersectional!

In the stunning rainbow deck and guidebook that is Ashley Molesso and Chess Needham's *The Queer Tarot*, the justice card is interpreted in this way: "Use this card as a reminder of the transformative power of collective action and the morals and values that guide you to seek justice."

This is the magick of the disabled community, in all our intersections. Together, we bring a rainbow of magick. This card declares our power and our belovedness. Our ability to individually and—most especially—collectively transform ableist spaces because our lives, our words, our actions, and our activism look at unjust systems and say, "There must be another way. For we exist."

If you draw this card, consider the following:

- In what ways have you been supported by the collective justice work of your disabled ancestors?

- In what ways do you support future and present members of the disability community?

- In what small ways can you infuse justice magick into your intentions for today?

52. Disability and Tarot: A Reading from the Hanged Man Card (Major Arcana 12)

Now we look at the hanged man card—which is one hell of a name! Skye Alexander's *The Modern Witchcraft Book of Tarot* lists both "letting go" and "sacrifice" as keywords associated with this intense pull. And I think both are possible ways of describing the experience of spoon allocation.

This card, with its extreme imagery, is an invitation for us disabled spoonies to acknowledge the power of cutting off, of killing, our allegiances to capitalist and ableist expectations, rooting out those ideas which come from unjust assumptions. And one of the most powerful ways to do that is by setting boundaries, acknowledging the number of spoons we have, and doing the work of self-care with as many of those spoons as we can.

If you pull this card, consider the following questions:

- What small (or large) commitments may need to be released in your current season of spoonage?

- What ableist expectations may have creeped into your intentions? What could you focus your energies on instead?

- In what small ways can you resist the pull of extreme capitalism by resting today?

53. Disability and Tarot: A Reading from the Death Card (Major Arcana 13)

And now the death card. By far one of the most fucking metal of tarot cards. But it need not provoke panic. For this card contains multitudes—just like you. One possible meaning of this card is "fear of change," according to Sahar Huneidi-Palmer in *The Book of Tarot: A Spiritual Key to Understanding the Cards.*

Disability is one of those things that forces humans to confront their mortality and their fear of change. Disability doesn't let you go on your merry, unsustainable, capitalist, ableist way. Oh no. Like death, it is no respecter of persons and takes no prisoners. It will change, it will transform, and it will come for you—for no one leaves this life without being disabled at some point.

Pulling the death card, in its fiery intensity, speaks to the unbridled magick of disability, with its ability to heal by crumbling the systems that aren't working to make way for more connected and kind ways of being. And the death card also says it's okay to grieve—to have big feelings as strong as death—throughout the whole change. (And, hey, as a Jesus-y witch, I know that you can't have resurrection without death.)

If you pull the death card, consider the following:

- In what ways might a radical change in your own life or activism help you to find a healthier rhythm, even if that change causes grief?

- What losses have you experienced as a disabled person in an ableist society?

- What are your feelings about these and other losses?

- Who are safe people you could process these feelings with, such as therapists or friends?

54. Disability and Tarot: A Reading from the Temperance Card (Major Arcana 14)

And now we pull the temperance card. In *A Little Bit of Tarot: An Introduction to Reading Tarot*, Cassandra Eason describes this as "the finding the balance card."

The walk of chronic illness and disability is one of finding balance in a unique way. You have dreams and goals that you want to achieve. You want to participate in your community. But you also have way fewer spoons and often way less money and time and more administrative work than the average non-disabled person does. Still, goals and dreams and community connections are so important to the human experience.

And so, the temperance card is an invitation for us spoonies to hold two things in tension: our need to rest and the things that take spoons but give life.

If you pull this card, consider the following:

- What are your dreams? Goals? Ways you want to connect more in your community?

- What are your spoons like in this season of life? What about other recent seasons?

- Where is there margin (or where can margin be made) to allow you to use some spoons for things that give you life?

55. Disability and Tarot: A Reading from the Devil Card (Major Arcana 15)

The devil card. Oh, the devil card. A little scary, a little campy, and very fascinating.

In *Young Oracle Tarot*, author Suki Ferguson interprets this card in relationship to difficult seasons where something feels wrong but the solution is yet to come. Ferguson assures readers that this "feeling bad" is fixable and "part of being human."

During low-spoon days and flare-ups, it can be so discouraging. You wonder, *Will it ever end? Will I ever get a diagnosis or treatment that helps?*

In a reassuring way, the devil card invites us to recognize the things that don't feel right, knowing that that feeling won't last forever and we are on the road to addressing the things that are giving us so much grief.

If you draw this card, consider the following:

- What are you feeling right now? What hurts? What emotions are you experiencing?

- What do you know about the symptoms or trials that are affecting you?

- What small things are you already doing to address them?

56. Disability and Tarot: A Reading from the Tower Card (Major Arcana 16)

The tower card scares a lot of people because of its meaning of sudden change. Michelle Tea, in *Modern Tarot: Connecting with Your Higher Self through the Wisdom of the Cards*, suggests an interesting interpretation for this intense card: "Either you or someone who impacts you has experienced a sudden clarity—a truly paradigm-shifting experience has arrived."

And if you're disabled, this can ring so true. Much of the disabled experience is "paradigm shifting" to us and those we interact with. And that magick is not something to be feared, but something to be honored for the wisdom and perspective it gives.

If you're experiencing a big life change, know that your magick remains intact and transformation through your disabled lens is possible for yourself and/or the people around you. Your existence is a mighty tower of power, standing strong in resistance to ableist systems and expectations. You are the paradigm shift.

If you pull this card, consider the following questions:

- How have you weathered sudden change in the past?

- How can you carry that same resilience and magick into any present or future changes?

- How has your disabled experience changed your perspective or the perspective of those around you?

57. Disability and Tarot: A Reading from the Star Card (Major Arcana 17)

We now move on to the uplifting star card, which is quite a relief if you're walking through the cards in order. It follows a series of super intense cards, like death and the tower.

The star card, by contrast, can refer to "hope" and "healing," according to Tina Gong's *Tarot*. And so, this card is a breath of fresh air, an invitation to dream and set intentions that are as cosmically glorious as you are. In other words, as disabled people, we can fucking reach the stars in our own damn way. Ableist society be damned, we are magick.

If you draw this card, consider the following:

- What things bring you hope? What things bring you healing?

- How can you invite those things into your life in small ways?

- What intentions can you set around these things?

58. Disability and Tarot: A Reading from the Moon Card (Major Arcana 18)

We now turn to the moon card, which might be one of my favorites in the whole deck (as the moon is a big part of my own witchy practice). In *Tarot for One: The Art of Reading for Yourself*, Courtney Weber describes the moon card as a signal of a "path . . . now better illuminated." If you're a disabled spoonie, this card might invite you to see the ways our symptoms and spoons illuminate the path forward to how we will express our disabled witchcraft.

Indeed, the moon's phases are analogous to the ebb-and-flow symptom experience of many spoonies. I wrote about this at *All The Threads*, my Substack newsletter:

The moon goes in phases, and my symptoms—mental, physical, and everything in between—go in phases. On days when it's bad, I remember that the brightness of a metaphorical full moon is on the rise. On days when it's good, I remember the importance of the darkness of periods of rest. On the really bad days, I remember that eclipses don't last forever . . . in a day, in a week, in a month, or maybe even in a year, things will feel better again. Through it all, the moon is still the beloved moon . . . and I am still the beloved me.

If you draw this card, consider the following questions:

- Consider the phases of the moon. What "phase" are your symptoms most like? Or are any of your disabilities more static?

- How might your symptoms and spoon levels be an invitation to you to change something?

59. Disability and Tarot: A Reading from the Sun Card (Major Arcana 19)

We now turn to the sun. This stunning card always fills me with a sense of beauty, wonder, and hope. And that's for a reason. In the amazing *Next World Tarot* by Cristy C. Road, the sun card is described as "raw enthusiasm and conscious levity."

This card invites us into joy and celebration. As disabled people, we are often viewed with only pity (at best). This card stands in opposition to that idea. Instead, the sun card says, "We are human. We are magnificent. We are magick. We have hopes. We have dreams. We have beauty. We have joy."

If you draw this card, consider the following questions:

- What things bring you high levels of joy?

- When was the last time you allowed yourself to be silly with abandon?

- What people and places make you feel safest to express the wildest parts of your joy?

- Where is it accessible for you to share wild joy?

- In what small ways can you infuse that wild joy into your everyday life and your witchy rituals?

60. Disability and Tarot: A Reading from the Judgment Card (Major Arcana 20)

The judgment card. What a loaded word. If you grew up in religious fundamentalism like I did, you know that the word *judgment* denotes disapproval and rejection from family, community, and even God. Even if you didn't grow up in this world, the word *judgment* can still strike fear into our hearts: fear of losing community or of facing unjust legal systems as disabled and otherwise marginalized people.

It's this complex meaning and background that I think makes the judgment card so interesting for disabled readers (and really any readers). In *Neo Tarot: A Fresh Approach to Self-Care, Healing & Empowerment*, author Jerico Mandybur notes this meaning for this card: "Your judgement of yourself or a situation will lead you to a game-changing realization."

And so this card is not an invitation to shame, rejection, exile, or injustice. Instead, it is about connecting to our inner wisdom, intuition, and magick. As disabled people, we are particularly adept and magickal at navigating unjust systems with the power of our judgment and intuition, transforming our communities and world.

If you pull this card, consider the following questions:

- What situations are you currently facing that require your judgment and magickal intuition?

- What knowledge, experience, and wisdom do you bring to this situation?

- What questions do you still have? Who are trusted people or resources you could consult about these remaining inquiries?

- How can you empower yourself to trust your judgment in this and other difficult situations? What intentions could you infuse in your rituals toward this goal?

61. Disability and Tarot: A Reading from the World Card (Major Arcana 21)

The world card is sweeping in visuals and meaning—a fitting way to close out the major arcana. Isabella Rotman's *This Might Hurt Tarot Guidebook* notes that this card may point to "self-actualization" and "the end of a cycle."

In other words, this card is a sweeping invitation to consider all that you have been learning and to crystallize lessons and wisdom from your experiences. If you've been walking through the tarot deck card by card, this might be an opportunity to consider what cards called to you the most during this point in your life. If you've been busy with lots of things, this may be an opportunity to look at what things are most aligned with who you want to be and what you want to spend your limited time and spoons on. If you've been in a slower season, this card might be an invitation to dream big about the present and the future. Either way, this magickal card is cosmic in scale—just like magnificent, disabled you.

If you pull this card, consider the following questions:

- In the ebb and flow of your days, have you noticed any patterns or themes in what you're learning?

- Which of these themes seem most aligned with your current spoon levels and goals?

- How might you crystallize that wisdom into short intentions?

62. Minor Arcana: The Wands

Now we move on to the minor arcana, which comprises four suits. The suit of wands signifies "action, initiative, invention, and energy."[22] It is an invitation to consider what you want and practical ways to get there. If you draw one of the wands, in addition to more specific wisdom from each of the cards within this suit, consider the following:

- What are your goals and dreams? (Think big here. These are not goals that have to happen overnight.)

- What are your current spoon levels? When do you notice they change?

- What are some small ways you could pursue the above goals with your current spoons? (Think of things that are truly small. If you want to write, consider making a goal of writing a sentence a day. If you want to make a career change, consider reading one article per day about what it takes to make that change. If you want to learn about a new side of witchcraft, consider a goal of listening to one podcast episode about that subject every week for a month. If you want to manage some symptoms in a new way, consider reaching out to one new provider—or doing some other small medical admin task—every other day.)

---

22 "The Minor Arcana Tarot Cards," accessed September 24, 2023, Tarot.com, https://www.tarot.com/tarot/cards/minor-arcana.

63. Minor Arcana: The Cups

The suit of cups signifies the many facets of challenges you may be facing, offering a space to "help you harness the strength of your own mind."[23]

In the swirl of doctor's appointments, misdiagnoses, prescriptions, treatments not covered by insurance, ebbing and flowing symptoms, working from minimal funds (because of capitalism and the high cost of healthcare), and more, the disabled life is one that is full of challenges. And this card is an invitation to find the resources surrounding us and within us, realizing we are not alone and that there is power within us and within our spoonie communities.

If you draw one of the cups, in addition to more specific wisdom from each of the cards within this suit, consider the following:

- If you've been given a cup of suffering recently, what are some resources that would be nice to have right now?

- If you've been given a cup of prosperity, how might you share your resources with others?

- What accommodations, resources, and community are presently available to you?

- What are the strengths within you at this time?

---

23 "The Minor Arcana Tarot Cards."

64. Minor Arcana: The Swords

The suit of swords is such a badass art collection—the stabby artwork depicted on these cards symbolizes witchy empowerment. Brittany Beringer, an astrology columnist for *Bustle*, notes that this suit "asks you to focus on logic and thought."

Drawing one of these cards might be considered an opportunity to get your witchy research hat on. To make reasoned and tight plans, essays, and goals. To keep to more structure than normal in order to challenge yourself.

If you draw one of the swords, in addition to more specific wisdom from each of the cards within this suit, consider the following:

- What do you know to be true about yourself, your world, and your spoons?

- What evidence-based treatments and strategies do you want to add to your routine to further your goals?

- How might you transform research into intentions for your magickal practice?

65. Minor Arcana: The Pentacles

The suit of pentacles is arguably the most witchy looking of the arcana, with the distinctive five-point star associated with witchcraft and Wicca. Brittany Beringer of *Bustle* notes that this witchy suit is "connected to the earth element, meaning [it] focuses on the material world."

This suit, then, could be interpreted as an invitation to consider your connection to nature and to pursue grounding practices that help you rest in your belovedness. To consider how, while an ableist world might attempt to alienate you from nature through lack of accessibility accommodations, you belong and are just as magickal as anything else in this earthy globe we inhabit in the interconnected cosmos.

If you draw one of the pentacles, in addition to more specific wisdom from each of the cards within this suit, consider the following:

- What small things make you feel connected to the earth?

- How could you turn these things into brief intentions? Rituals?

- What things make you feel disconnected from nature as a disabled person? What accommodations might be available to you?

These prompts will help you as you journey through the individual cards within the suit of pentacles.

66. Making the Tarot Your Own: Crafty Rituals for Spoonies

In this chapter, we've gone over the major arcana and even touched on the suits that make up the minor arcana. That's a lot of wisdom and witchy loose threads with lots of potential. How to bring it down to the practical and holdable?

As you can probably guess, I love to use art rituals for figuring out this path from the cosmic to the mundane, and so I've included some ritual prompts to help you pull from the tarot those things that are most meaningful and magickal for you. Then you can write your story with tarot.

The major arcana is often described as a story in itself, showing the journey of the fool through each of its twenty-two cards. As a writer, I really connected with this idea; I love a good writing prompt for destroying writer's block, and story is kind of my life's work. Consider the following prompts to help you write your story through tarot:

- Go through each of the major arcana in their traditional order. For each card, write one sentence about how it applies to your own life story as a disabled person. You could make this visual in some way, using stickers, ephemera, special items in a shadow box, colored pencils, paints, markers, or any other supplies you have.

- If you've recently gone through the whole tarot deck, think about what cards connected with you the most. Consider making your own version of the fool's journey in your own order in a way that reflects your life and experience, especially as it relates to disability. You could also add a visual component to this, using whatever art supplies you have.

- Consider making a banner of your most meaningful tarot cards and hanging it up in your house, tying them together with string in a pennant banner style. Or prominently display your most meaningful cards in your altar space.

Chapter Eight: Relationship Rituals

*T*won't rehash here how important community is to us as humans, but I will say that being disabled often requires a special kind of community reliance and participation. Our needs demand to be met, and we alone cannot always meet them, which is true of all humans but particularly hard to ignore in disability. These rituals invite you into a conversation about community and its connections to witchcraft and disability.

67. Invoking the Power of Marginalized Ancestors

Disability can be an alienating and lonely experience. But, ultimately, it's also a basically universal one. At some point, we will all be disabled.

And yet still, those of us who are disabled currently are sidelined and often unable to participate in our communities, even though we make up those same communities.

That's why I take comfort in invoking the power and even the love of my own disabled ancestors, hoping the next generation will be able to do the same toward me. I know there is disability in my family tree, both by accounts I've received from living relatives and just by sheer probability.

What would it look like to find strength in their power, their courage, their resistance-by-existence, even if I don't know them by name?

I wrote the following incantation with that in mind.

[• • •]

What You'll Need for This Ritual:

- A candle (or accessible alternative) with a correspondence meaningful for you, signifying drawing in strength, and/or love

- Accessible objects that represent your relevant ancestors (photos, notes from them, their favorite objects or foods, items in a color that evokes them, a drawing of them, a digital Pinterest board of pictures that remind you of them, etc.)

Before you begin, consider the following questions:

- What do you know about your ancestors? Do you know any of the disabilities they lived with?

- Disabled or not, do you know how your ancestors resisted through their existence? Their spirituality? What did their practices mean to them?

- How could you learn from their experiences? What would you do differently than they did and why?

Light or visualize the candle. If possible, arrange the items that represent your ancestors around the candle. Then repeat this incantation seven times, verbally or silently if your voice is not available.

> *I call in the love, the power, and the support of these my disabled or otherwise marginalized ancestors, [name them here if you know their names]. I honor and thank them for their resistance, their struggle, and the ways they found joy, experienced care, and expressed love. Today and always, I invoke their power. Their love, their existence is connected to me, and this too is magick.*

68. Incantation of Self-Love before Sex

Ableist messaging would have us believe that we the disabled are anything but sexy. But, as we have seen together, we are magickal and therefore sexiness is available to us just as much as it is to non-disabled people. But the wear and tear of health admin, chronic pain, and inaccessible environments—as well as internalized ableism—can make us begin to hate ourselves, which is a hindrance to both our self-worth and our sex lives. But we are worth having fulfilling sex lives filled with self-love.

Whether you're masturbating by yourself or enjoying spicy moments with a partner or partners, know that your disability, while it may require creative accommodations, does not bar you from expressing yourself sexually, if that is something you desire. Ultimately, all you need is consent, an awareness of your own needs (and the needs of any partners), and a sense of your own worth. That's where a self-love incantation comes in.

Before reciting it, consider the following questions:

- What are you interested in sexually? What things/ideas/actions/settings make you feel sexy?

- How can you find outlets for your sexual expression that are consensual and accommodating of your disability needs?

- What ableist notions about your own desirability or worthiness are most prominent in your mind?

- How might you turn these assumptions on their heads, transforming them through new ways of thinking and being as yourself?

Now recite the following incantation:

I am fucking magickal . . .

And that includes my sexuality.

As a disabled person, I transform ableist expectations and create new ways of finding pleasure for myself and any partners.

*I love myself and am a good lover of myself and
any partners that are involved.*

I look for ways to express that love.

*I listen to my needs and desires and the needs
and desires of any partners that are involved.*

*I establish consent; I am more aware of these
things as a disabled person because of the ways
I have been marginalized.*

My power and magick apply to sexuality.

*I am magick, regardless of my level of ability or
spoons.*

*I am fucking magickal . . . and magickal at
whatever fucking means to me.*

69. Empathy Incantation

I love the way Kendra Cherry, MSEd, describes empathy
on Verywell Mind: "the ability to emotionally understand
what other people feel, see things from their point of view,
and imagine yourself in their place."

As a spirituality so invested in the connection of all
nature, witchcraft is an excellent springboard for empathy.
Witchcraft also uses so much visualization, so imagining
the perspective of another is baked into our practice. And
as disabled people, our experiences of invalidation and

lack of understanding of our day-to-day accommodation struggles make us extra aware of the perspectives of those who are not usually heard.

I firmly believe that empathy is one of the greatest forms of resistance that we can use against injustice. If we understand the person we're supposed to see as the other, we might be able to find connection and even positive change where everyone's needs get met.

That's why I wrote this incantation.

> *I have lived experience as a disabled person. I*
> *invoke my power to empathize with not being*
> *heard. I cast my love as a spell over the world,*
> *toward all who are unheard that all may be*
> *seen, invoking not just my own love but the love*
> *of all who have gone before, all who love now,*
> *and all who will come after. In this power, I call*
> *in resistance. I call in my magick.*

70. Found Family as Ritual

Found family has been central to my spiritual experience—I am a queer, witchy exvangelical after all. In an article for *Psychology Today*, Jeremy Nobel, MD, MPH, compares the development of found family to gardens and vines: "[Chosen families] grow together like vines climbing the side of a house in summer: One day, you look up and realize they've bloomed, and there are simply too many to count."

This is green witchery if I've ever heard it! And it fits well into the transformative framework of disabled witchcraft too. When we're marginalized, we often make something (in this case, community) out of nothing, transforming ableist systems by creating alternative networks of true support.

This ritual is about thinking about the people who are already a part of your chosen family and considering what you dream of for that chosen family's future.

[• • •]

What You'll Need for This Ritual:

- Pictures or physical objects that represent your found family

- A place to house these items (sketchbook, picture frame, shadowbox, bin, etc.)

Begin this ritual by considering the following prompts:

- Who do you consider to be a part of your chosen family?

- With what people do you feel safest? Why?

- What do you consider to be a healthy chosen family?

- What characteristics and values are important to form and nurture that growing community? (For example, in an interview for Healthline, Bahiyyah

Maroon, PhD, suggests, "Start by asking yourself, 'What can I do to better show up for the people in my life who I care about?'") Who are trusted people you could talk with about this, such as friends, therapists, or other experts?

For the second part of this ritual, create a digital or physical collage or collection of pictures, words, colors, and/or objects that represent your current chosen family and/or what you see as the values undergirding your relationships with others. Infuse these values with intentions as you place the items onto the page or into the box, invoking your own power to be a gardener and green witch through your care for yourself and others in your chosen family.

Chapter Nine: Rituals for Getting through It

Y**ou are magickal, but frankly, on a low-spoon or even just a discouraging day, it can feel like nothing works to propel you toward meeting your needs. And that sucks because our system is so broken that we often can't take a day to rest. This chapter includes rituals for getting through life in general (which includes bad days) and navigating unjust healthcare systems—from starting new medications to finding humor to channeling anger and much more. In the pages to come, you'll find rituals to empower and express your magickal, witchy, spoonie self at every step of the journey.

71. Pulling Cards for Spoon Allocation

Have you ever heard of decision fatigue? Registered psychotherapist Natacha Duke, MA, RP, defines it as "a phenomenon (as opposed to a diagnosable medical condition) where the more decisions a person makes over the course of a day, the more physically, mentally and emotionally depleted they become."[24]

As a disabled person, I run into decision fatigue so fast. In addition to having less energy than non-disabled people have in a day, I have to do all the normal adult things (working, paying the bills, cleaning the house, making

24 "8 Signs of Decision Fatigue and How to Cope," Cleveland Clinic, June 1, 2023, https://health.clevelandclinic.org/decision-fatigue/>.

food, buying food, etc.), plus all the additional admin my diagnoses require (health insurance/bill wrangling, keeping track of medications and symptoms, managing new symptoms and all the doctor's appointments that requires, managing my regular doctor's appointments, etc.), all while figuring out which ones I should prioritize in case I run out of spoons.

Making decisions is important but not always possible when you have to make so many.

Using oracle decks of some kind (or divination of any kind) can help you make those decisions. I use oracle decks as a sort of prompt to consider what I need to do in a day. Often, I even create mantras based on that morning's card that help me make the decisions that aren't immediately obvious and thus take more brainpower (read: spoons) that I don't have.

The general, non-disabled public arguably does this too. For example, there was the 2021 "Is it a no-bones/bones day?" phenomenon on TikTok, where Noodle, a pug, was held up by their human as a form of divination: "If Noodle stays upright, then congratulations! It's a bones day! These are lucky days for taking risks and treating yourself. But if Noodle collapses, then it's a no-bones day, a sign it's best to take it easy."[25]

To perform this ritual, select your divination tool of choice. In this case, I'm recommending tarot cards, which

25 Sara M. Moniuszko, "Is It a 'No Bones' Day? Here's What That Means," USA Today, October 23, 2021, https://www.usatoday.com/story/life/health-wellness/2021/10/23/no-bones-day-heres-what-means/6138309001/.

you can find individual readings for in chapter seven. For spoon allocation, with whatever card you draw (or whatever divination tool you use), consider the following questions:

- How does this card invite you to care for yourself today?

- Is this card inviting you to rest more today or to use your limited spoons toward a limited number of must-dos?

- Is this card inviting you to seek additional help from others? What resources might this card remind you to take advantage of?

- How can the wisdom of this card remind you of your own worth, strength, and beauty?

- As a disabled person, how is the act of making your own decisions in this moment a way to transform and resist systems that work against your autonomy and safety?

72. Incantations for When You Can't Get Out of Bed

As a spoonie, my ability to write ebbs and flows. As I'm penning this particular ritual, I feel okay. But last night, I couldn't sleep because of the symptoms. And while I managed to get out of bed today, some days I just can't. Some days I get a good night's sleep and still struggle.

Other days, it's easier and I *almost* feel "normal" (I hate that word).

We need to make space in our communities for it all. Capitalism says to get up, push through, until the day you die.

We witchy spoonies resist with a resounding "Fuck no." We resist by staying in bed when our bodies need us to. What power we have in that reality!

Capitalism says the only power is in hoarding wealth and pulling ourselves up by our bootstraps and working ourselves quite literally to death.

But we know this isn't true. We have the real power. We can effect change simply by lying in our beds when that is what is needed.

Below I've written three incantations: one for getting out of bed when you are forced to, one for choosing to stay in bed when you need to before a crisis point of symptoms, and one for the days when you wake up with an unexpected level of symptoms that requires you to stay in bed.

Incantation 1:
Today, I was forced to get up when my body was not ready, when I needed to rest. I call a curse upon the unjust system that caused this. I also call upon my own power and magick by listening to my body and letting it call the shots, and by refusing to give my all to a system that demands more than anyone should ever have to give. This is my power.

Incantation 2:

Today, I resisted by [state your action: calling in, canceling plans, etc.]. I remained in bed before a crisis point of symptoms, and I used my power to set a boundary to increase my power for later. I honor my right to make these choices, and I stand in gratitude and awareness of any privilege I have that allows me to do this. I invoke this power for myself so that others—indeed, someday all people—can have the same rights. Today I invoke the magick of changing expectations, interrupting ableist norms.

Incantation 3:

Today, I have no choice but to stay in bed. I invoke my power to listen to my body. I invoke my right to do so. I call upon the love of all who have gone before, all who are here today, and all who will come after to support me in this healing magick. Today, I refuse to give my all to a system that demands more than anyone should ever have to give. This is my power.

73. Crystals for Nervous System Regulation

Crystals are a big conversation in witchcraft, and witches have a lot of complex thoughts and beliefs about how they can be used or how they work. For me, crystals are a focusing tool. I don't necessarily attach metaphysical meaning to them beyond the symbolism associated with them or the intentions I infuse into my rituals with them.

I live with PTSD from religious trauma, which means I'm often emotionally dysregulated and need grounding. So my most powerful use of crystals has been as a tool for nervous system regulation.

But what is nervous system regulation?

It means being aware of the ways we become activated and unable to function when our body goes into fight, flight, or freeze. It means finding ways to show our bodies we are safe because we are our own advocates, helping our bodies become rooted in the present and able to respond rather than react.

Early in my PTSD journey, I discovered crystals. Something about their beauty, their connection to earth, and their coolness to the touch gave me a sense of safety when very little else could, moving my body from a freeze response into the ability to move again.

There are many ways to integrate crystals into your nervous system regulation practices. Unfortunately, in a world stuck in capitalism, the crystal industry is rife with misinformation, low wages, dangerous working conditions, and ridiculously high prices for some rocks.

There's no easy answer about how to procure crystals ethically and economically, but I firmly believe that a rock gathered from your driveway, or given to you from your rockhound friend's collection, or purchased as a cooling facial roller from a discount store, or procured as a thrifted crystal bracelet, can be infused with meaning and magick.

If you're looking for a tool for nervous system regulation, here are two different iterations of a ritual that I use, usually in preparation for a stressful day. As always, I'm not a doctor or a mental health professional. If you're dealing with PTSD or similar mental health struggles, please work with your mental health professionals to determine what practices are a good fit for your particular needs.

[• • •]

What You'll Need for This Ritual:

- Crystals of your choice (see above for some procurement options)
- A small satchel and/or an outfit with pockets
- Crystal bracelet(s)

Hidden Satchel Crystal Ritual
Find a small satchel or bag and place crystals with the desired correspondences in it. Hold the satchel in your hands and reflect on the love and safety that the earth gives you, feeling the coolness of the stones. Place the satchel in your pocket and carry it with you. During the day, if you are feeling anxious, go to a quiet place (if possible) and reach into your pocket, resting your hand on the satchel to ground yourself.

Crystal Bracelet Ritual

Select a crystal bracelet or bracelets with the desired correspondences. Place the bracelet(s) on your wrist(s) and feel the coolness of the stones, reflecting on the love and safety that the earth gives you. During the day, if you are feeling anxious, go to a quiet place (if possible) and rub the crystal bracelet(s) in a circular motion (or any motion that feels grounding), being sure to pay attention to the coolness of the stones and the intentions you've placed in them.

74. Possible Rituals for Doctor's Appointments

When I'm experiencing particularly severe symptoms, it's not unusual for me to have four medical appointments per week. And that's assuming I'm in a position to afford medical appointments.

And with that much driving around, sitting in waiting rooms, accompanying insurance and payment admin, and prepping to advocate for myself (especially with new providers), it's really hard to get a moment to ground myself through spiritual practices.

I've developed the following rituals for when you have a few minutes of quiet in the waiting room. Please adapt them for your particular needs and situation:

Ritual Idea #1: Keep a small oracle deck and/or journal in the bag you bring to medical appointments (and/or keep digital versions of these on your device). Pull a card while sitting in the waiting room and journal about your feelings about the card and how it might connect to your experience visiting doctors. Consider: How might you invoke your own power in this situation, using the creative prompt of the card?

Ritual Idea #2: Visiting a provider can be scary. Try this self-advocacy incantation for the waiting room: "Today, no matter how I am treated, I will treat myself well. I will use whatever voice I have and advocate for my needs. There is no right or wrong here, only care. I honor myself and I invoke the love of all who have gone before, and all in the present, and all who will come after to rest in that love and to call upon any medical providers to also rest in and express that love through their work. This is the magick of self-advocacy, and this is my power.

Ritual Idea #3: Use the hidden satchel crystal ritual and/or crystal bracelet ritual (from #19) to ground yourself at an anxiety-inducing appointment.

Dear witchy spoonies, may you find power even in our capitalistic medical system. You are magickal, and you are transforming a broken system by your very presence.

75. A Curse upon Unjust Health Systems

I'm going to be honest with you. I rarely use curses in my practice. And when I do, I aim them at unjust systems, not humans. I'm a Christian witch, so I consider my curses to be a form of imprecatory psalms, which are a type of prayer found in the Bible asking or demanding that God enact justice against an oppressor.

One of the most obvious oppressive systems that disabled witches run up against is the healthcare system. Capitalism makes it so we can't afford the care we need . . . and the care we do receive is given by overworked and often underpaid healthcare workers, many of whom have not received training in trauma-informed care and may not be up to date on the research about chronic illnesses (which are notoriously understudied, likely because they are common in marginalized populations).

I see the harm this system inflicts on so many individuals, and so I pray and curse against it. I invoke every power I have access to—both in the hopes of creating miraculous change and as a way to propel myself forward, running headlong into the unjust system with my spiritual spoonie siblings and raising hell, trying to transform it for the good of all.

So today I write this curse out, inviting all who read it to join me in this prayer, this invocation, this curse against that which is unjust . . . as we imagine a better world for the future.

Start by lighting a black candle (or accessible alternative with similar correspondences) for banishment and protection, and then say the following:

> *A curse upon the unjust healthcare system.*
> *A curse upon corporate greed. A curse upon*
> *misinformation. A curse upon medical bias*
> *against the marginalized. A curse upon laws*

which seek to criminalize and destroy healthcare options. A curse upon one-size-fits-all solutions. A curse upon medical gaslighting. A curse upon abuse of the patient-doctor relationship. A curse upon insurance companies, who have abandoned people to die in poverty. A curse upon misdiagnosis that leads to further harm. A curse upon whatever harms are as yet hidden from me due to my own bias.

I call upon the love and connection of the universe to destroy these unjust forces and transform them into life, joy, reparations, health, abundance, knowledge, wisdom, safety, community, freedom of expression, equity, and wholeness for all. I call upon that power to propel me, my spoonie siblings, and our allies forward toward a just world for all.

76. A Ritual for When You Must Create One More Spoon

We've all been there. The day is drawing to a close, but your responsibilities in an inhumane system are not. The time for rest is near, but there is still at least one task left to do, even though there are few to no spoons left to do it with.

This is a ritual for these moments. And because this ritual is for when you have no spoons, I'm keeping this one nice and short, with little to no prep.

[• • •]

What You'll Need for This Ritual:

- An actual spoon (or an accessible alternative or visualization)

Put your body in a relaxing position. Hold the spoon up to your body (either physically or in your mind's eye) and imagine your energy and its energy connecting to each other. Repeat the following incantation.

> *I invoke my power to create one last spoon for one last task today. I am enough, whether or not I have a spoon left. I will care for myself in this last task and only do what is absolutely necessary. And then I will rest as soon as possible. This is my power.*

77. Self-Compassion Spell

This book is about resistance, but I never want it to be about perfection. The fact of the matter is that disability uniquely requires us to assess our priorities and to live in a state of radical self-compassion, regardless of productivity.

Negative self-talk can be so detrimental to our sense of worth, especially when we're living with bodies that—in a pronounced way—can't meet the inhumane expectations of capitalism. That's why I think a positive spell has so much power. Self-compassion gives us the opportunities to extend the same kindness to ourselves that we might extend to others. When the Wiccan rede says, "Do no harm," that means harm to yourself too.

[• • •]

What You'll Need for This Ritual:

- A favorite food or drink item, such as tea or a cookie

- Items that remind you of yourself (or visualize these items if that would be more accessible); include things you love about yourself (representations of your hobbies, interests, skills, happy memories, etc.) and things about yourself that you struggle to hold space and kindness for

After you take a drink or a bite of your chosen snack or beverage, repeat the following words:

*I am enough, and I call upon the love
undergirding and connecting the universe
and all elements. I bask in self-compassion on
productive days and low-spoon days. I hold
all of me in love and patience, trusting my
ancestors and the earth to hold in love all parts
of me that I can't yet hold in love for myself.*

> *At all times and at all energy levels, this is my*
> *power to claim.*

Then, finish your snack or beverage, reflecting on these words as you savor what you are consuming.

This spell might bring up a lot of feelings, so give yourself lots of space to process and safe community to process with, such as trusted therapists or friends.

I'll say it again: you are enough, dear witchy spoonie. Now treat yourself in self-compassion, trusting this spell to do its work. Because you are the power behind it, by your very existence.

78. Cleaning Spells: To Be Recited When Cleaning on Days with No Energy

If you're a spoonie, you know the kind of day . . . the one with no energy, when symptoms are high and the stress is raised, and yet there's cleaning to do. And if you have intersecting diagnoses, this can get even more overwhelming, especially when it comes to those taking-care-of-yourself things that do you good but are just out of reach.

On days like this, I remind myself that cleaning is not about perfection, but is instead a ritual of caring for myself and anyone who lives with me. It especially helps to view it as a ritual. Here's one version of that ritual that may be helpful to you too on those cleaning days with no energy.

[• • •]

What You'll Need for This Ritual:

- A broom or any other accessible cleaning implements needed

- A timer

Before beginning, take the broom or other cleaning implement and hold it close to you. Visualize some of your energy, even if it's just a tiny amount, going into the item. Then, recite the following spell:

> *O broom [or other cleaning implement], today*
> *I connect my power to you, to clean for care*
> *and not perfection. Enable me to take small,*
> *impactful steps of care in my cleaning routine*
> *today. Whatever I can do today is enough. I*
> *transform my limited energy into this care task.*
> *My cleaning is magick. My care is magick. I am*
> *magick. And I am enough.*

Set a timer for a very short amount of time to clean before resting, depending on your own personal spoon levels. Repeat the spell as needed while completing what you need to, being kind and generous with yourself as to how much cleaning you get done.

79. Emergency Wonder: A Ritual of Favorite Things

Disability in an ableist world can be unbelievably discouraging. One reason I love witchcraft is that it is one of the ways I connect to the wonder and joy of life, even when systems and diagnoses push against me.

Some days, though, that weight causes me to be so low on spoons that I can't find the energy to do even the simplest of witchy spiritual care for myself.

On these days, I turn to the ritual of emergency wonder. I first wrote about this concept on *All The Threads*, my Substack newsletter. This is how I defined this practice: "Basically, 'emergency wonder' is any practice that requires very few spoons and results in an instant sense of wonder and hope. Emergency wonder includes any practice that works for all phases of chronic illness: the full moon of good days, the eclipse of flare-ups, and everything in between."

Emergency wonder can be anything you have on hand that is easy and can literally be done on no spoons. My emergency wonder kit includes:

- A jar of plastic butterflies I bought in bulk. They are in a rainbow of colors and just arranging them or pouring them out of the jar is so beautiful, it always makes me feel a bit more hopeful.

- Thrifted art and coffee table books. I love flipping through beautiful art and photo books, as well as old art/DIY magazines. You can thrift these very cheaply at most thrift stores or at library book sales. And, for an absolutely free option, most libraries (including digital options like Hoopla and Libby) have some on hand at each branch and/or available to be placed on hold and brought directly to your branch. If you have a bigger budget, you can even buy newer ones at your local bookstore. Currently, my roster includes books about floral arrangements (with gorgeous photo spreads that don't cause migraines for me, like in-person flowers often do), books about cute creatures, and a whole host of old crafter magazines from circa 2012.

- Holding a crystal or other special rock.

- Spreading out tarot cards or other oracle decks.

When you've found those things that bring you hope just by looking at them, put them in a place where they are easy to access. When you need some emergency wonder, grab your preferred item or items and recite the following incantation:

> *Wonder is resistance. In the midst of discouragement, I hold up beauty. I transform the space I inhabit into one of wonder, hope, and change. My body has connected me to the healing power of beauty by drawing my eye to these physical reminders. I gather the energy of*

joy from them and transform that energy into
hope and even action for myself. This is my
power.

80. Coping Incantations for Bad Pain

You know the pain days that are so hard that you can barely think straight? While they are not my every day, they are a regular reality. Mild to moderate pain is, in many ways, the norm for me, but sometimes the levels reach exceptional heights.

When all medical options have been exhausted, I've found two witchy incantations to be helpful.

First, I call on my guides. For you, that might be deities, saints, the love of family members, the love of friends, or the love of ancestors:

> *[Name], be with me. Uphold me. Help me with*
> *my pain. Be with me in it. I call on your power*
> *and love. Remind me that I am not alone and*
> *not without power or support, even in the midst*
> *of pain.*

Then, I call upon my body through honor and gratitude. Pain is the body's way of communicating with us, and while it isn't always clear what the body needs, pain is an opportunity to listen to your body's wisdom and cries and validate them (and, by extension, yourself). I say something like this:

> *I see you, body. I hear you. Your power in*
> *communication is strong, heard, and even*
> *welcome. I don't know the solution, but I honor*
> *you. I will rest as much as I can. I will find*
> *magick in your communication. I will find love*
> *in your signals.*

This is not a solution to pain, but it does help with the coping side. And when I'm less panicked, I'm in less distress than I otherwise would be. Know you are not alone, dear spoonie—your guides, your in-person community, and even your care team are here, and your body is communicating with you even now. You are powerful. You are strong. You are magick. And you are enough.

81. Fuck!: Angry Incantations

Swearing is fucking magickal. And it's powerful.

As disabled people, we see so much injustice and feel so much pain. And sometimes there is nothing more accessible and more cathartic than swearing. In fact, there was some lovely research published in 2020 about swearing as a pain reliever, finding "a 32% increase in pain threshold" for participants who swore.[26]

---

26 Richard Stephens and Olly Robertson, "Swearing as a Response to Pain: Assessing Hypoalgesic Effects of Novel 'Swear' Words," Front Psychol 11 (2020): 723. doi:10.3389/fpsyg.2020.00723. PMID: 32425851; PMCID: PMC7204505. https://www.ncbi.nlm.nih.gov/pmc/articles/PMC7204505/

In a capitalist society with so little free access to pain management methods, it's nice to know that my very body can provide some relief simply by saying *fuck*.

Essentially, this ritual is about swearing in response to pain, injustice, what-have-you—using powerful words to do a form of spellwork. Because I can think of few human words with as much intention and power packed into them as swear words.

So, if you're low on spoons and/or not able to say some kind of grandiose or verbose spell, try channeling your energy into the swear word of your choice. Let its strength show your power.

It's enough. Because you're fucking magickal.

For this ritual, reflect on these questions:

- Consider your favorite swear words: What feelings and intentions do they evoke?

- How might your favorites function as correspondences? For instance, I like to use *bullshit* to channel energy against ableist assumptions. I like to use *fuck* as a correspondence for power and challenging taboos and unjust structures.

- How could this swear-y energy be channeled into your magickal practice on low-spoon or otherwise stressful and overly taxing days?

Now that you've considered the above, visualize your word of choice and the power and correspondences you associate with it. From the energy of that word, imagine unjust systems crumbling and new, more inclusive ways of being springing up. Carry this image with you, and swear with your word of choice whenever you need a little anti-ableist magick throughout your day.

82. Spell of Sillies

There's an old cliché: laughter is the best medicine. But if you're disabled or otherwise marginalized, a saying like this might feel really unhelpful, just like all the other unhelpful things people say when they just don't get it:

- Well, just smile more and you'll feel better.

- This disabled person is *so* joyful. Why can't *you* be inspiring like them?

- Oh, look how happy you are today. You're an inspiration. No accommodations for you because you clearly don't need them.

It's maddening. But what if we reclaimed laughter in the witchy way only we can?

If humor is about subverting expectations, what if we embraced the things that make each of us weird and silly and unique? What magick might ensue?

For this ritual, consider the things that make you laugh and the things that make you feel like yourself.

Gather things that represent humor to you (or simply visualize them). Think about what it is about them that makes you laugh. What does it feel like? Channel that silly energy into the items and the space around you. Then, repeat the following words:

> *I laugh in the face of attempts to crush me and my community. I laugh, not because there is no injustice or because I am callous, but because laughter says I am worthy of joy and that that joy is enough on its own. I invoke this power against unjust and ableist systems. This laughter is a spell, magick from my very self.*

83. Incantation: Holding Space for Yourself

There's so much ableist messaging to internalize in our world. One of those messages that I internalize so much is the idea that I am taking up too much space—just by having needs.

It's fucking ridiculous how capitalism has so alienated us from our bodies and communities that we genuinely are made to believe that our communities would be better off if we didn't share our needs and self-expression with each other.

But us magickal spoonies, we know that this lie—this idea that we should shut up and not communicate our needs or wants because we're disabled and an inherent burden—is bullshit.

All of this is why I wrote the following incantation. Sometimes, so much gets in the way of our literal and figurative voices. However you communicate your needs and wants, this incantation is for you.

> *I take up space. I honor my needs and wants by expressing them. In this way, I not only make space for myself but also do the same for others, creating a culture in which everyone has the opportunity to participate, express themselves, and share their needs and wants. This is magick. This is power. This is community. And I invoke all of these as I step forward to care for myself (and by extension others) by communicating my needs.*

84. Grounding Spell for Bad Days

So I live with PTSD from religious trauma. Grounding is vital for me, and it was only natural that it should fit into my witchy practice as a disabled person.

Crystal Raypole, a writer for Healthline, defines grounding this way: "a practice that can help you pull away from flashbacks, unwanted memories, and negative or challenging emotions . . . that may help you refocus on the present moment" with one common example being "techniques [that] use your five senses or tangible objects—things you can touch—to help you move through distress."

A quick disclaimer here: I am not a therapist. I'm just a person with PTSD. If you're dealing with this or any other mental health concerns, please reach out to a trusted mental health professional and work with them to find practices that work for you.

One of my favorite grounding techniques is to feel the earth under me. This can work whether I'm sitting down and my feet are touching the ground or I'm lying down and I can find the ground (or my bed) beneath me.

This grounding spell connects these ideas to the four elements: earth, water, air, fire.

The best place to do this, if you want to physically act out the spell, is in the kitchen, where you have access to items that represent each of the four elements in a safe, accessible, and convenient way. Otherwise, you can visualize each step.

Say the following words while performing the accompanying actions:

I feel the earth.

(Connect your feet, hands, back, or other part of yourself to the ground or to whatever you are resting on, which is itself connecting to the earth.)

I feel the water.

(Turn on your faucet and run water over your fingers or gently splash water onto your face, making any accommodations you need for your body.)

I feel the fire.

(For safety, turn on your faucet and run warm—not hot—water over your fingers or gently splash water onto your face, making any accommodations you need for your body.)

I feel the air.

(Stand in front of a fan or vent or open a window just a bit to feel the air.)

I invoke my connection to all through these four elements. I am loved, I am powerful, I am magick, I find true safety through my connection to all and the resources provided therein.

85. Questions Brew

This one goes out to all my religiously traumatized spoonies. I wrote about self-compassion in spiritual practices at my friend Aly Prades's Substack newsletter, *A Glitch in the Good Enough*, where I talked about one of the most healing things I found on my religious trauma journey: "One of the most helpful and healing things

I've ever done is just sitting with the questions I have, especially about religious things—acknowledging that I don't have all the answers and sitting with that fact."

We exist in a society that is ableist and so difficult to live in. There are so many unanswered questions about why we as humans keep letting suffering continue. No matter your religious beliefs or labels (or lack thereof), it's totally natural to have questions.

That's why I developed this ritual—to process those things that are just without answers.

[• • •]

What You'll Need for This Ritual:

- A jar or bowl
- Paper
- Water
- A writing utensil

Start by taking some time to write down your questions on strips of paper, being gentle with yourself as you do. Once you have done that, fill the bowl or jar with water. Then drop each question into the jar. Place the jar in sunlight or moonlight for twenty-four hours. Once the twenty-four hours is over, remove the paper scraps and dispose of them as you see fit and as is accessible to you, repeating the following:

I receive the love of the sun, of the moon, of all who have gone before, and of [any relevant deities/guides], knowing this love is present with me, even in the midst of unanswerable questions. I express compassion to myself in not knowing and in grieving whatever losses have come. I am enough, and I rest on my community as I process the feelings that come with questions.

86. Sweeping Ritual

In her 2019 video "Doing a Witchy House Cleaning,"[27] YouTuber Corinne Leigh talks about her own witchcraft practice and performs several rituals in an instructional fashion. The most moving for me is her sweeping ritual, where she sweeps a room where a traumatic event happened. 2019 was an extremely traumatic year for me for a lot of reasons, so I found great healing in this sweeping ritual.

Corinne says, "My main meditation during this sweeping process was visualizing sweeping away the trauma."

I have used similar rituals so much since watching this video, even procuring a special corn broom for this purpose (from a big box hardware store because of my disabled budget, but someday I hope to get one of those gorgeous handmade, ethically produced witchy brooms

---

27 https://www.youtube.com/watch?v=5hg6dKYehxI

from Etsy). But it doesn't have to be a major traumatic event. It can be anything that you want to sweep out. I often use it when someone has said something toxic or abusive (or ableist or all three) to me and I can't get it out of my head. Sometimes, I even light a black candle for banishment and set that in my altar, repeating internally or out loud as I sweep:

I banish this bullshit. I am worthy and magick.
With my power, I sweep this out of my space
so it can be transformed and absorbed by the
earth's love, never to harm anyone again.

87. Ritual before Seeing a New Provider

One of the most quietly hard things about being disabled is the regular engagement with new healthcare providers. It can be for any number of reasons: a provider goes out of practice, a new symptom or diagnosis emerges (requiring a new specialist), a provider is unkind or abusive (and you need a new one), a provider goes out of network, or you move to a new city where the cost of living is cheaper.

Whatever the reason, our minds swirl with valid and justified fears. Will this provider really see me? Will this provider believe my condition exists? Will this provider be collaborative in my care instead of approaching it in a hierarchical way, where they assume they know everything about my experience because they have a medical degree?

This ritual is meant to be empowering to you as you enter these new spaces.

$$[\bullet\bullet\bullet]$$

What You'll Need for This Ritual:

- Two candles, one black and one red (or accessible alternatives with similar correspondences)

Before your appointment, light a black candle for banishing fear of what could be (including the real possibility of ableism). Then, light the red candle to call in self-love, self-compassion, and all the available compassion in the medical space you will be entering.

Repeat the following words:

At this appointment I banish fear of all the ableism that may surround me. I call in self-love, self-compassion, and all the available compassion from all who have gone before, all who are in this medical space, and all who will come after, to empower me to declare my needs and for them to be heard. I am enough and worthy, regardless of outcomes, and I will use whatever resources I have to receive care, resting and advocating in rhythms that make sense for me. I am magick and will transform my ableist surroundings simply by being present.

88. Ritual for Starting a New Medication

Taking a new medication can be scary. You're figuring out what resources will work for your body, balancing side effects and symptoms. This is transformative work that your body is doing, and this ritual is meant to honor that.

Surround yourself with items that have correspondences of love, care, and hope. Then, relax your whole body and repeat this incantation:

> *I attempt this medication as a form of magickal self-care, working in community with my care providers to honor this body's difficult road in an ableist society. I will listen to my body and advocate for it throughout this whole process. I will be in touch with my community about how I am feeling and will be gentle with myself as I get used to this possible new rhythm. I am magick, and I am enough.*

Take the medicine as directed by your care provider. Then, do something that makes you smile or laugh or feel comfortable to take your mind off any anxieties: watch a favorite movie, invite some friends over, play a game, make art, etc.

As you assess your symptoms in the time frame given by your care provider, staying in touch with them and continuing to be gentle with yourself, know that you are taking steps in magickal self-care and that you are in charge of how you care for your body. You've got this, my fellow witchy spoonie.

89. Ritual for Reproductive Care

I'm writing from the US, and living in a post-Roe world is scary for someone with a uterus. But restricted access to reproductive healthcare affects us all. It's not just about abortion—it's about comprehensive sex ed, birth control access, treatments for reproductive diagnoses (like endometriosis and vaginismus, just to name two of my own), the way gender-affirming care interacts with reproductive healthcare, and general healthcare access for all.

All of these are difficult enough to get, even when you are able-bodied. They are often expensive and life changing even if you're privileged with an above-average amount of wealth. And as spoonies, we face so many additional obstacles: lack of money to pay premiums, co-pays, and bills; extra shitty health insurance coverage (or no coverage) because of pre-existing health conditions; having to travel obscene distances to providers with little to no transportation options; having to take time off of work to make it to appointments, exacerbating all of the above problems; and the list goes on and on. Add in all the post-Roe bullshit restrictions and the way our other diagnoses can interact poorly with pregnancy, and you've got a terrifying recipe for horrific outcomes that can disproportionately affect the disabled community.

And that's why I wrote the below ritual. I wanted to create a spiritual space for processing, existing, and resisting when we inevitably do need to seek reproductive care.

[• • •]

What You'll Need for This Ritual:

- Music that helps you feel centered, calm, and/or empowered

- Any other grounding tools that work for you (such as crystals, stress balls, ice water, fans, etc.)

- A candle (or accessible alternative) that represents correspondences of love, safety, and power

Start by turning on your music of choice and using any other grounding tools you love. Then, light the candle. Once you've set everything up and centered yourself, repeat the following words:

> *I am magick. Today, I seek magickal self-care for my body in the form of reproductive healthcare. I transform a lack of resources by invoking my own power, along with the love, power, support, and resources of my community—past, present, and future. I seek out whatever I can procure for my needs in this moment, knowing that I am resourceful, a*

practitioner of the strong disabled witchcraft.
This resourcefulness, this creativity, this insight
from my experiences is my power. I am enough,
and I am magick.

P.S. Here are some resources for reproductive healthcare:

- Legal Helpline: Call 844-868-2812 or visit ReproLegalHelpline.org today for legal advice and information on abortion in your state.

- How to avoid fake clinics that do not offer abortion: https://abortionfunds.org/how-do-i-find-the-clinic-thats-right-for-me/

- Need funds? The National Network of Abortion Funds may be able to help: https://abortionfunds.org/need-abortion/

90. Kitchen Ritual for Dietary Restrictions

The kitchen is supposed to be a warm and nourishing place, but for disabled people, it can often carry traumatic ableist associations. Many of us (myself included) live with dietary restrictions, and I've found this is a very challenging concept for able-bodied people to grasp. And in this haze of confusion and assumptions, we as the disabled community are forced to constantly explain concepts like reading food labels extra carefully, cross contamination, and the differences between allergies and intolerances. It's exhausting, and often only results in gaslighting: "I'm sure you'll be fine." "It's just a little garlic/gluten/dairy/what-have-you." "I'm sure this seasoning doesn't have what you're talking about."

And then there's the fact that many of us aren't able to cook for ourselves at all, or at least in the ways that we want to.

For these reasons, I called in the help of a little kitchen witchery to create a ritual to heal our relationship with the kitchen space. To transform it into a place of empowerment rather than exclusively a place where missteps have hurt us in significant ways.

[• • •]

What You'll Need for This Ritual:

- Three candles: one white, one black, and one red (or accessible alternatives with similar correspondences)

- A kitchen utensil of some kind

To begin, light the white candle and say, "I call in my own power, sense of safety and self-advocacy, and creativity."

Then, light the black candle and say, "I banish those ableist assumptions that have caused me to feel unsafe or unloved in my own kitchen or in the kitchens of my loved ones." If you want, you can name the assumptions you're thinking about individually and, after each one, declare, "I banish you."

Then, light a red candle and say, "I call in the warmth that a kitchen is supposed to have by calling upon the love of all who have gone before, all who are present now, and all who will come after."

In the glow of the candles, hold the kitchen utensil of your choice close to your heart and visualize your energy and power flowing into it. Then, repeat the following:

In me is earth, water, air, and fire. I call in all my power to show myself self-love and self-advocacy in the kitchen. I consecrate this space as a place of learning, healing, and nourishment, where I have the power to create good food for myself and others and where I have the power to educate others when they may be operating from ableist assumptions. May this kitchen be reclaimed as a place of hope and possibility and protected from any ableism that may try to sneak in. I am magick, and I am enough.

Conclusion: A Blessing

*A*nd so we reach the end of this journey, but not the end of the path.

I hope in these pages you've found the magick inside of you and adapted or even transformed any ritual that calls to you.

I hope that you've found new ways to see your beauty and to send up a beautiful "fuck you" to ableism in all spaces, including the spiritual ones.

I hope you've discovered a deeper sense of belovedness, of connection to community in and around you.

I hope you've felt seen—as a valuable, vibrant, and fucking fabulous and magickal being.

I hope you've unearthed space for yourself, your experiences, and your dreams where there wasn't space before.

I hope that, in these pages, you've found new ways to resist, new ways to be authentically you.

Wherever you started this journey and wherever you are leaving it—and with whatever sexual orientation, gender identity or expression, religious/spiritual label (or lack thereof), socioeconomic status, race, or ability you hold—I hope you go on knowing that you are magickal and that the path is expansive and the future so bright.

And so I close with a blessing for us all.

My dear witchy spoonies, you are enough. Take what you want and leave what doesn't serve you from these pages. And don't let anyone ever fucking tell you that you are anything less than magickal. Like earth, water, air, and fire, you have power and resistance in your very existence.

Recommended Resources

Witchcraft and Nature-Based Spiritual Practice Resources from BIPOC Voices:

- *The Altar Within: A Radical Devotional Guide to Liberate the Divine Self* by Juliet Diaz

- *Witchery: Embrace the Witch Within* by Juliet Diaz

- *The Seasons of the Witch* oracle decks by Juliet Diaz and Lorraine Anderson

- *You Are the Medicine: 13 Moons of Indigenous Wisdom, Ancestral Connection, and Animal Spirit Guidance* by Asha Frost

- *Braiding Sweetgrass: Indigenous Wisdom, Scientific Knowledge, and the Teachings of Plants* by Robin Wall Kimmerer

Tarot Resources & Decks:

- *Kawaii Tarot: Understanding Tarot with the Kawaii Universe* by Chris Barsanti, illustrated by Lulu Mayo

- *Tarot: Connect with Yourself, Develop Your Intuition, Live Mindfully* by Tina Gong

- *Cozy Witch Tarot Deck* by Amanda Lovelace, illustrated by Janaina Medeiros

- *This Might Hurt Tarot Deck* by Isabella Rotman

- *The Modern Witch Tarot Deck* by Lisa Sterle

Witchy History Resources:

- The Witch: A History of Fear, from Ancient Times to the Present by Ronald Hutton

- The Goddess Obscured: Transformation of the Grain Protectress from Goddess to Saint by Pamela Berger

- "A Dress Historian Explains the History of the Witch Hat," a video essay by Abby Cox

Because We Talked about Sex Magick—Some Good Sex Ed Resources for a Variety of Experiences:

- A Quick & Easy Guide to Sex & Disability by A. Andrews

- You Know, Sex: Bodies, Gender, Puberty, and Other Things by Cory Silverberg and Fiona Smyth

- Bang!: Masturbation for People of All Genders and Abilities, edited by Vic Liu

- Open Deeply: A Guide to Building Conscious, Compassionate Open Relationships by Kate Loree, LMFT

- PlannedParenthood.org

- Hannah Witton's YouTube channel

Other Witchcraft Resources:

- *Utopian Witch: Solarpunk Magick to Fight Climate Change and Save the World* by Justine Norton-Kertson

- *The Practical Witch's Almanac* by Friday Gladheart

Acknowledgments

*T*o all the love that holds up the universe and connects us all

To the love of all who have gone before, all who are present, and all who will come after

To my guides: Father, Jesus, Holy Spirit, Mother of Us All and all the saints/beloved dead, most especially my disabled, witchy, and queer ancestors

To my nesting partner, Kevin; to my rad weirdo, Maria; to my roommate, Jenn; and to all my other found family (your love, care, and support throughout this process has meant the world)

To my local libraries and bookstores for all of the sources you connected me with and support you've given me

To the team at Microcosm for taking a chance on this passion project and for giving this book wings

To my reader and writer friends at *All The Threads*

To anyone else who helped make this book a reality

To all you beloved witchy spoonies,

You are all fucking magickal.

SUBSCRIBE!

For as little as $15/month, you can
support a small, independent publisher
and get every book that we publish—
delivered to your doorstep!

www.Microcosm.Pub/BFF

BE THE PERSON YOU WANT TO BE AT MICROCOSM.PUB